RICH

The 27 Manifestations of Balance

R. R. Bennett, Sr.

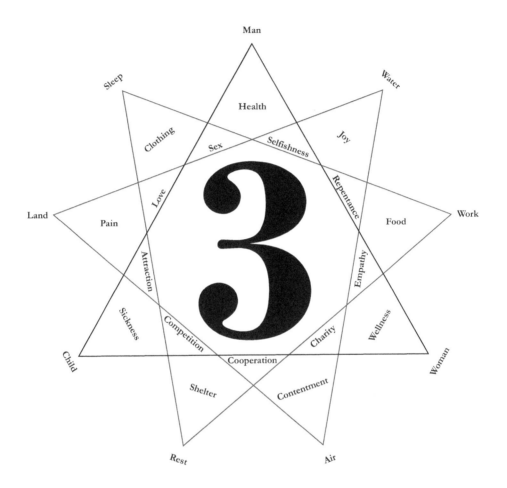

Man

Sleep

Water

Health

Clothing

Joy

Sex

Selfishness

Repentance

Love

Land

Pain

Food

Work

Attraction

Empathy

Sickness

Competition

Charity

Wellness

Child

Cooperation

Woman

Shelter

Contentment

Rest

Air

UNITYSTAR

"For though I am free from all men, I have made myself a servant to all, that I might win the more; and to the Jews I became as a Jew, that I might win Jews; to those who are under the law, as under the law, that I might win those who are under the law; to those who are without law, as without law (not being without law toward God, but under law toward Christ), that I might win those who are without law; to the weak I became as weak, that I might win the weak. I have become all things to all men, that I might by all means save some. Now this I do for the gospel's sake, that I may be partaker of it with you." - Apostle Paul[1]

"Nothing is wasted if you take nothing for granted."

R. R. Bennett, Sr.

About the Author

    R. R. Bennett, Sr. is an American Life Enrichment Coach and an avid reader who was born during the height of the civil rights movement. An Independent Author (Authorpreneur) of both Fiction and Non-Fiction in the genre of Life Enrichment, he believes that we are not in the universe, but that the universe is in us. Therefore, all that you need starts from within you. He also believes that people don't grow old and die, but rather, they stop growing and die. R. R. Bennett, Sr. is an Autodidact who understood the power of reading early in life. Abraham Lincoln, Fredrick Douglass, and Maya Angelou are 3 of his fellow Autodidacts he most admires. He feels that one of the most fascinating things in the world is that with only the twenty-six letters of the Roman Alphabet so many different things can be said in an infinite number of ways. He thinks that the *Holy Torah*, *Holy Bible*, and *Holy Quran* are the 3 most powerful books this world will ever know. He feels that *Think and Grow Rich*, *The Purpose Driven Life*, and *Rich: the 27 Manifestations of Balance* are the 3 books that everybody should read at least once in their lifetime. He resides in Upstate New York and lists his job and his hobbies as one and the same: exercising, reading, writing, speaking and teaching. His signature statement is "love love, hate hate."

"I'm just a poor man telling other poor people where the bread is."

"Better to have God than Luck because Lucky only comes to visit but God comes to stay."

"In a storm do you see God or a Ghost? In your answer lies your faith."

R. R. Bennett, Sr.

Table of Contents

Introduction

Rich: The 27 Manifestations of Balance is a book and a guide to help you balance your life so that you can live a rich life. This book is divided into 27 chapters, and I recommend that you read only one chapter a day for 27 consecutive days and review the previous 3 chapters you have read every 3rd day.

On the front cover of this book is a diagram of the Unity Star. The Unity Star is made up of nine points (primary), nine spaces (necessary) and nine inner pyramids (secondary), together representing the twenty-seven manifestations of balance in the human life that are required to be rich. To be rich is to be in union with the universe, which will lead one to have high value as an individual. The words universe and unity operate as a union of fairness and oneness, which is the original call for all of mankind to balance the world.

However, one must realize that balance can only be achieved with the appropriate combination of variety and unity. In other words, we achieve and appreciate balance by "weighing up" the variety in our life that gives us the single answer of unity. With unity, like with balance, there is harmony. The first portion of the "harmony formula" expresses diversity. The second portion expresses unity. Though people are born differently, the Spirit of the Universe's work is unified. In other words, if you are the work of the Spirit of the Universe, you will deliver peace.

Black is the color of formality.

Green is the color of fertility.

Red is the color of desire.

The Unity Star is formed by overlapping 3 large triangles, one black, one green, and one red. The black triangle represents the formal-spirit of the family, the green triangle represents the fertile-soul of the world, and the red triangle represents the fire, the energy, and the blood of the desiring-body in which we live while on this earth.

The number 3 represents balance. I have not found any number in this world other than 3 that even comes close to representing balance and its unifying power of mutuality, and I believe the many points made in this book will have the reader come to that same conclusion.

The number 3 represents the black people, the brown people, and the white people. Although many people also include the labels of red and yellow people, my firm belief is that they also are brown people. The number 3 represents the past, the present, the future, the positive, the negative, and the neutral. It also represents the Father, the Son, the Holy Spirit, and the 3 Abrahamic religions of Judaism, Christianity, and Islam.

There are 3 main relationships in life: your relationship with self, with others and with the Spirit of the Universe. There are 3 degrees of living: almost living, most living, and utmost living.

There are 3 levels of creation: the world of visible, the world of psychological, and the world of invisible. The world of visible is everything you can see. Our five senses are in place to navigate this first world. The world of psychological is everything you think and feel, which includes your thoughts, desires, dreams, and fears. Our mind and body are in place to navigate this second world. The invisible world is something of its own where only spirituality exists. It takes spiritual awareness to be able to navigate this third world.

Because there are more than ninety-nine names for God, in this book, I will use the name Spirit of the Universe, in order for me to have the ability in this book to educate many people from many spiritual backgrounds.

The Spirit of the Universe is the beginning of all and the end of all. How the Spirit of the Universe reveals Himself to you is as unique as your own individual mentality. Therefore, there are many ways to the Spirit of the Universe, because we are many people. At the end of the day, there is only one Spirit of the Universe. I believe the bell of liberty is ringing, that we are one people, in one world, under one Spirit of the Universe, and it is understanding that oneness of us all that has the ability to dissipate any tensions that arise during interfaith talks.

The Bible states that Jesus Christ was 30-years of age when He began his ministry and He engaged in a 3-year ministry. Christ was 33-years of age at the time of His crucifixion, and He rose from the grave on the 3rd day.

The number 3 also represents the 3 percent of the world's people whose lives are balanced and who know how to teach other people to balance their own lives; they are the righteous teachers of humanity. Ten percent of the world's people live balanced lives but are not teachers; they are the role models of humanity. Sixty percent of the world's people are coachable when it comes to the process of universal balance. However, only one-third of these people will ever apply what they learn and live a balanced life. Twenty-seven percent of the world's people will never care to live a balanced life. When you combine that number (twenty-seven percent) with the forty percent of people who did not apply what they learned, sixty-seven percent of the world's people will live an unbalanced life. 33 percent of the world's people will either be students, role models or teachers of the process of balance, which is required to live a rich life.

So let my message of the "Philosophy of Balance" in this book be heard, not only in spiritual study but in the barbershop and the beauty salon as well. You are the only expert in your entire life who truly knows who you are and what you need to be balanced. Every day we, as individuals, decide to add to or subtract from our lives, with each of these decisions having the ability to balance or unbalance our lives. Only you can recognize what it takes to balance your life. I am simply the expert in the coaching process of achieving balance, which is required in order for you to live a life of enrichment.

Through my many years of adventures, I have wrestled with the meaning of life. I have never settled for someone else's answer, but through my experience and study of the whole range of human possibilities, I have come to realize that the profound insight of life is to be balanced, and that balance is the only true way to be rich. To be rich in life you must have a balanced life.

"Honest weights and scales are the LORD's; All the weights in the bag are His work." (Proverbs 16:11)[1]

All the money in the world will not make you rich. To be rich is to live life abundantly in need of nothing. People with a lot of money commit suicide because, in reality, they were broke, the very opposite of rich. A balanced person is rich, needing nothing, and will never willfully stop the journey of life by committing suicide. A rich life is a joyful life.

If you are not taking the time to balance your life, then in your life there will be holes. Too many people try to fill those holes in their lives with the wrong things, such as sex and drugs, instead of repentance and love. You must fill the holes in your life with the treasure of life and not the trash of life. You can't put anything anywhere, and you can't do anything anytime. If you want your life to be balanced, then you must put it in order.

Our universe responds to our thoughts, words, and actions. We strive to accumulate, to gain, to move up the ladder, to end up with the most of everything that we can, only to find out that our "things" are running our lives, instead of the other way around. When we become too busy, we are unbalanced and out of order, and we confuse activity with productivity.

Order is the number one law of the universe. We are not in the universe; the universe is in us. You are all that is. The Spirit of the Universe is closer to man than his own jugular veins. The love of the Spirit of the Universe is always in the midst of us, whether seen as the free flying bird who decided to share the podium with Senator Bernie Sanders as he delivered his speech, or the young boy who ran onto the court during the game to give NBA superstar Carmelo Anthony a hug.

We only need to look to see the love of the Spirit of the Universe. If we stay in tune with the universe, we stay within our natural selves, and by that, we stay in order. When you put your life in order, you get rid of everything that isn't directly related to life's order, and you end up with just what you need, which you probably had all along, buried underneath everything you don't need. It is a process I call addition by subtraction. Sometimes you need to sacrifice what you are for what you can become. If we stay in order, we become balanced. When we are balanced, we become rich, and when we are rich, we need nothing. In fact, when you are rich, boredom is an emotional state that you fail to participate in because rich people always have something meaningful to do and something meaningful to live for.

There is nothing more important in a human life than balance. In today's world, it's easy to lose yourself, but when you are balanced, it is nearly impossible to be lost. Money can't buy you balance, but balance can earn you money. Balance will make you strong, safe and free; not free to do as you please, but free to put your life in order.

Everything created by the Spirit of the Universe contains a set of invisible instructions. These instructions allow you to determine exactly what you were created to do so that you can fulfill your purpose on this earth. We are not born with a set of neatly printed instructions, but they are there just the same, invisible, ready and waiting for us to discover them. It is up to us to figure out what those directions say and then follow them.

Everything in nature was created for either bad or good. In general, we should work towards increasing the good and decreasing the bad. However, it takes wisdom to understand that sometimes by removing the bad, you produce something worse than bad. So pay close attention when removing what you perceive to be bad.

If you do not bend your soul to any one particular voice, but rather, listen to all the voices, then you will hear the great voices of the universe speaking one single word, and that word will be order. Where there is order, there will be balance, and where there is balance, there will be peace. These 3 go together: order, balance, and peace. You can't have one without the other because all 3 define the word harmony.

With respect to financial capital, when we spend too much money, we run up debt, which if left unbalanced, will eventually result in bankruptcy. With human capital, when we draw down too much from our very self, we also run up a debt which needs to be balanced.

A poorly balanced human is not only a personal liability but a social liability as well. Poorly balanced people are more prone to unemployment, drug abuse, and violence, which ultimately makes it more difficult for these people to sustain themselves. In harmony, there is no violence.

Working against humanity by over exploiting human capital can be catastrophic, first regarding personal loss, second regarding household productivity, and finally, the very community itself is at risk of a total collapse. In a very real sense, your environment is your extended body. The world will not be destroyed by the wicked, but by the cowards who refuse to stop them.

You went through a process to become unbalanced in your life. Therefore, you must go through a process to become balanced in your life. A balanced person will become successful, but it will require work. The only time success comes before work is in the dictionary. You must work first to have success later. Balancing your life is possible as long as you understand and respect the natural order of life.

First, you have to break the thought pattern of only thinking about me, myself and I. This might not be easy, however, it is necessary and highly worth pursuing. Second, you must break the trance of materialism. Breaking from thinking only about self and materialism is an awakening from mental imprisonment. The balanced person, by definition, lives beyond the habitual boundaries of the alienated, self-centered person.

The balanced person feels as empathetically present in others and all that is around them as they do in themselves. Your soul is the entire world. Therefore, you must understand that experience is not what happens to you; it is what you do with what happens to you.

Every place you've ever been and everything you've ever done is school, and it is up to you to learn as you travel through the classes of life. Balancing your life is a lifetime process and a true education, which ultimately leads to a rich life.

The purpose of attending to your life is to support the state of being balanced. Transformation is the rule of life; nothing in the universe stands still. Therefore, you must always work to remain balanced. I see a balanced life as an opportunity for greater wisdom, love, meaning, joy and increased mental and physical capacity.

As you begin to balance your life, you will begin to claim the ability to tap into your inner self and the possibilities of your unlimited energy, creativity and vitality, and by doing so live a purpose driven life. You will feel better and function better as a human being. A balanced life is a purpose driven life and a rich life.

There are some who think that life on Earth is Hell. Nothing could be further from the truth. There is no ministry in Hell. Ministry is for the living. It is we human beings who have the ability to smell the lingering scent of divinity. A doubter always wants to be told there is no such thing. Therefore, it is important for us to be aware of those who deny, deflect and demonize.

I was called by the Spirit of the Universe in the year 1984. I was prepared in the wilderness by the hardship of life and His word. For 3 decades I remained His pupil, receiving revelation after revelation. He provided for me, protected me and got me moving in the right direction. I went from a son of man, to a child of God, to a man of God, which is the natural progression of living on the righteous path of life.

I tried it the wrong way, and I don't know anyone who gave it a better shot at doing it wrong than me. I know what it is to be walking around like the blind, deaf and dumb. I was dead, too dead even to lay down. If there is a man on this earth that the Spirit of the Universe has taken better care of than me, I would like to meet him.

It is only by the Spirit of the Universe that I was able to be dragged through the mud and still come out clean. And now, there is no doubt in my mind that His law and order, which has been set forth for all of mankind to heed, leads to a balanced life, which is required to be rich.

There is a difference between being rich and being wealthy, and you can be one without the other. However, the aim of this book is to show you how to be rich, which will allow you to handle wealth properly, should you ever acquire such status at some point in your life.

There are 3 different types of awareness needed to live a rich life: self-awareness, political awareness and financial awareness. There are only two kinds of money problems: too much money and not enough money. You need to be aware in order to find your balance.

You can have the world's greatest software, but if you install it on a computer that has a faulty operating system, the results will be disastrous. Being balanced allows us to take in and delete information properly. More times than not, it's not the software that's the problem, it's the operating system. It's not the world that's unbalanced, it's the people operating in the world that are unbalanced. The world is a balanced and rich place to those who are balanced and rich. However, it is important that I make this final point; absolute balance means stasis, and stasis means inactivity. Only when the scale of balance tips in one direction or another can the seesaw of life keep moving.

Although I write with facts and a touch of poetry, I also teach with doctrine, because it is my hope that every written word in this book will help you to become who you were created to be: balanced and forever rich. In other words, I don't teach people how to become wealthy; I teach people how to become rich. Simply put, my "Philosophy of Balance" is the formula for living rich.

Love Love, Hate Hate.

May the Spirit be with you,

R. R. Bennett, Sr.

Primary

Man

: an adult male human being
: a man or boy who shows the qualities (such as strength and courage) that men are traditionally supposed to have
: the human race: humankind[1]

Man is the beginning of the human being. The male chromosome, or Y chromosome, is passed down identically from father to son, so mutations, or point changes, in the male sex chromosome can be traced through the male line back to Africa and to Adam, who is the father of us all.

"And The LORD God formed man of the dust of the ground, and breathed into his nostrils the breath of life; and man became a living being." (Genesis 2:7)[2]

"Let us hear the conclusion of the whole matter: Fear God and keep His commandments, for this is man's all." (Ecclesiastes 12:13)[3]

A man is obligated first and foremost to love the Spirit of the Universe. Therefore, his prayer should be the first thing he does when he awakens from sleep.

"Now in the morning, having risen a long while before daylight, He went out and departed to a solitary place; and there He prayed." (Mark 1:35)[4]

Man must love himself but must also come to the understanding that he was not born for himself alone. Man is the head of the family, and therefore, he should provide and protect not only for his family but also for the well-being of planet earth. It's important to keep order and balance.

"But I want you to know that the head of every man is Christ, the head of woman is man, and the head of Christ is God." (1 Corinthians 11:3)[5]

"Watch, stand fast in the faith, be brave, be strong. Let all that you do be done with love." (1 Corinthians 16:13-14)[6]

Man represents the sun. The sun and man each have great significance. They both signify father and represent individuality and the energy of production, which initiates all action. Without the sun, our solar system would not exist; it is the force of life. Without man, our family structure will not be in balance because he is the foundation.

The sun is very important when considering the health of an individual. It rules key aspects of our nutritional needs. We need the sun to produce vitamin D and plants need the sun in order to grow and become food not only for us but also for animals as well.

Man is very important when it comes to the health of a family; he rules woman and child. In fact, being a husband and father is the most honorable part of life for a man. It is man's duty to cultivate and improve those gifts which he finds within himself and contribute all that lies in his power to the benefit of the universe.

Every man has so much enlightenment in himself that with the necessary care and due consideration, he will come to understand the natural order of balance. Man must fight against all people, places, and things that try to unbalance him. Sure, he may become unbalanced at times, but the fight to be balanced must always remain within him.

To become balanced is a process that starts with the man. Man must learn how to be a man by a man. Just like iron sharpens iron, man sharpens man. There are 3 stages that a man should come to understand in his life: how to be a son, how to be a husband and how to be a father, because this wisdom must be passed on to the next generation. It is also by this wisdom that his manhood (Kingdom) will be established.

Any man, in need or not, should have a job. A man should not waste his time by not doing anything. He should spend his money on the well-being of his family. All extra monies should be given to charity, to those in need. Extra money for one person is not the same as extra money for another. You need to figure out for yourself when it is that you have crossed that line.

Man will (and must) desire a need for money and things since he must have them for his own well-being as well as to fulfill his duty to provide for the well-being of the woman and children in his family.

A wise man should never let his enemy see his hand. The wise men of the world are those who listen to the Spirit of the Universe first, and then to their women, be it wife, daughter, mother, or sister. Every man who seeks power and money increases his chances of getting those things by having the right woman at his side. The most important business lesson a man can ever learn is that if you want to be rich and wealthy, you must understand that having the right woman by your side is more important than an MBA. Since money and things are of a very perishable nature and may be taken from a man without warning, a man must, with respect to money and things, put his life in such a balanced state that he will not lose his mind if he should happen to lose his money.

A man must always give into the modest demands of restraint and temperance. It is incumbent on man, in order to improve and to become well balanced, to use the utmost diligence to gain mastery over money, sex, and things. Criminal monies must always be avoided, and honor over money should always be the mindset of a man. A balanced man should not pervert justice, should not show partiality, and should not take a bribe. A man should display love, which is the first of the nine attributes of the fruit of the Spirit.

"But the fruit of the Spirit is love, joy, peace, longsuffering, kindness, goodness, faithfulness, gentleness, self-control. Against such there is no law. And those who are Christ's have crucified the flesh with its passions and desires. If we live in the Spirit, let us also walk in the Spirit." (Galatians 5:22-25)[7]

Man must take care of his physical body with the proper food and exercise. Man must not ruin his body with excessive eating and drinking. There is a time to leave the parents and let every man have his own wife because the joining of man and women is of the natural order.

> Have you not read that He who made them at the beginning, "made them male and female," and said, "For this reason a man shall leave his father and mother and be joined to his wife, and the two shall become one flesh?" So then, they are no longer two but one flesh. Therefore what God has joined together, let not man separate. (Matthew 19:4-6)[8]

> "He who finds a wife finds a good thing, And obtains favor from the LORD." (Proverbs 18:22)[9]

> Husbands, love your wives, just as Christ also loved the church and gave Himself for her, that He might sanctify and cleanse her with the washing of water by the word, that He might present her to Himself a glorious church, not having spot or wrinkle or any such thing, but that she should be holy and without blemish. So husbands ought to love their own wives as their own bodies; he who loves his wife loves himself. For no one ever hated his own flesh, but nourishes and cherishes it, just as the LORD does the church. For we are members of His body, of His flesh and of His bones. "For this reason a man shall leave his father and mother and be joined to his wife, and the two shall become one flesh." This is a great mystery, but I speak concerning Christ and the church. Nevertheless let each one of you in particular so love his own wife as himself, and let the wife see that she respects her husband. (Ephesians 5:25-33)[10]

A man should not permit his wife's interest in him to die. A great wife should know how to cook or be willing to learn. It is a disgrace if she cannot or will not cook because a family dish prepared with her own hands is just about as soul food as food can get. A great wife is a woman who loves you, supports you, cooks, cleans, loves to be a mother to her children and is willing to put up with your character flaws - we all have character flaws. A great wife is smart, warm-hearted, and not self-centered in any way. The greatest gain for a man is a faithful woman who, when she sees him, becomes happy and protects his property and her honor in his absence. Stay away from women who only care about themselves, constantly voice their opinions, are materialistic or always seem to be in competition against you.

"Better to dwell in a corner of a housetop, than in a house shared with a contentious woman." (Proverbs 21:9)[11]

There is no need to be sleeping with the enemy. Your wife should know better than to spread gossip or reveal pillow talk (private conversations between a husband and wife). Your wife must be your most loyal soldier. She should not work as an assistant or secretary unless her boss is a woman. In other words, a great wife will not work at a place where she feels like she has to look pretty because men are around.

What a man hears, reads and sees will be what a man thinks. It will require some discipline to filter what a man hears and sees, however, what a man reads, for the most part, is entirely up to him. The mind thrives on the dominating thoughts that are fed to it; you are what you eat.

Because there are seven days in our week, the number seven represents the seven days of the week in each of our years of age. As a rule of my wisdom, I recommend that a man should choose a wife whose age is no less than fifty percent of his age plus seven years. A man must understand the women is his helpmate, and should never bring shame or harm to the spirit, soul or body of the woman.

A man with a high sex drive should come to understand sexual-transmutation, which is to take the downward outward flow of sexual energy and transmute it into an inward upward flow of creativity. In spite of the fact that men are polygamous by their biological nature, every man reaches greater heights when he has the right woman by his side. The pitfalls of gluttony, drunkenness and sexual immorality must be avoided. A man with the right courage will not fall into such pitfalls, thus giving himself more life, while the man who lacks such courage will give himself less life. A man must be aware of toxic masculinities. In other words, put away your childish ways and be a man.

"When I was a child, I spoke as a child, I understood as a child, I thought as a child; but when I became a man, I put away childish things." (1 Corinthians 13:11)[12]

> But now you yourselves are to put off all these: anger, wrath, malice, blasphemy, filthy language out of your mouth. Do not lie to one another, since you have put off the old man with his deeds, and have put on the new man who is renewed in knowledge according to the image of Him who created him. (Colossians 3:8-10)[13]

There are many ways men and women differ. There are the more obvious physiological differences between a man and a woman (for example, a man is generally fifty percent stronger than a woman), but most of these ways we are not even aware of. Here are nine of those differences:

1. Females normally outlive males by 3 or four years in the U.S. Females simply have a stronger hold on life than males, even in the uterus.
2. More than one hundred and forty male babies are conceived for every one hundred females; by the time birth occurs, the ratio is one hundred and five to one hundred, with the rest of the males dying in spontaneous abortions.
3. Men have a higher incidence of death from almost every disease except: benign tumors, disorders related to female

reproduction, and breast cancer.

4. Men have a higher rate of basal metabolism than women.
5. Boys' teeth last longer than do those of girls.
6. Women have a larger stomach, kidneys, liver, and appendix, and smaller lungs than men.
7. Female lung capacity is about thirty percent less than in males.
8. Women have 3 very important physiological functions totally absent in men - menstruation, pregnancy, and lactation. Each of these mechanisms influences behavior and feelings significantly, making women more responsive emotionally, by laughing and crying more readily.
9. All things being equal, men are fifty percent stronger than women in brute strength.
   Men and women differ in every cell of their bodies because their chromosomal pattern is different. The implications of those genetic components range from obvious to extremely subtle.[14]

No man has knowledge of everything, however, when a man is ignorant of the great value of the Spirit of the Universe as well as indifferent towards the needs of his family, it will result in his own shame and his own loss. As the saying goes, "a rolling stone gathers no moss." Papa need not be a rolling stone. His relationship with the Spirit of the Universe and the blood harmony of his family is sacred. Man must do his best to provide for and protect the woman and the children as long as he has breath in his body, all the while living an honest and sociable life.

No sober and considerate man will ever deny the truth of reasoning which he comes to for the ministering of justice and liberty to all. Man must learn to be comforted within himself with the testimony of a good conscience and with the assurance that his integrity is in balance with the Spirit of the Universe. I will say it again. Man must learn to be comforted within himself with the testimony of a good conscience and with the assurance that his integrity is in balance with the Spirit of the Universe.

Every sin is a sin of dishonor. There are Ten Commandments, the first four deal with dishonoring the Spirit of the Universe and the last six deal with dishonoring people.

And God spoke all these words, saying:

I am the LORD your God, who brought you out of the land of Egypt, out of the house of bondage.

You shall have no other gods before Me.

You shall not make for yourself a carved image—any likeness of anything that is in heaven above, or that is in the earth beneath, or that is in the water under the earth; you shall not bow down to them nor serve them. For I, the LORD your God, am a jealous God, visiting the iniquity of the fathers upon the children to the third and fourth generations of those who hate Me, but showing mercy to thousands, to those who love Me and keep My commandments.

You shall not take the name of the LORD your God in vain, for the LORD will not hold him guiltless who takes His name in vain.

Remember the Sabbath day, to keep it holy. Six days you shall labor and do all your work, but the seventh day is the Sabbath of the LORD your God. In it you shall do no work: you, nor your son, nor your daughter, nor your male servant, nor your female servant, nor your cattle, nor your stranger who is within your gates. For in six days the LORD made the heavens and the earth, the sea, and all that is in them, and rested the seventh day. Therefore the LORD blessed the Sabbath day and hallowed it.

Honor your father and your mother, that your days may be long upon the land which the LORD your God is giving you.

You shall not murder.

You shall not commit adultery.

You shall not steal.

You shall not bear false witness against your neighbor.

You shall not covet your neighbor's house; you shall not covet your neighbor's wife, nor his male servant, nor his female servant, nor his ox, nor his donkey, nor anything that is your neighbor's. (Exodus 20:1-17)[15]

Your future will be determined by whom or by what you honor. All blessings come through a chain of authority. Success is a product of honor and failure is a product of dishonor.

A man should be an example to the world in 3 ways: in conversation, in behavior and in purity (both in sexual matters and in thoughts). A man should be honest, just and straight in every daily matter in all his dealings, not only with other people but also with himself, in his obedience to the natural order of the Spirit of the Universe.

As long as my breath is in me,
And the breath of God in my nostrils,
My lips will not speak wickedness,
Nor my tongue utter deceit.
Far be it from me
That I should say you are right;
Till I die I will not put away my integrity from me.
My righteousness I hold fast, and will not let it go;
My heart shall not reproach me as long as I live. (Job 27:3-6)[16]

"You shall do no injustice in judgment, in measurement of length, weight, or volume. You shall have honest scales, honest weights, an honest ephah, and an honest hin." (Leviticus 19:35-36)[17]

"Let me be weighed on honest scales, that God may know my integrity." (Job 31:6)[18]

"Dishonest scales are an abomination to the LORD, but a just weight is His delight." (Proverbs 11:1)[19]

Justice keeps the human world balanced, but alcohol and recreational drug use disturb man's judgment. Alcohol and recreational drug use are some of man's biggest problems. Alcohol and recreational drug use disconnect man from his natural self. Without alcohol and recreational drug use, man can maintain a balanced attitude and stay balanced in both success and failure. With a balanced mind, man pulls through difficult times. It is very important for a man to balance his attitude, for a balanced attitude brings harmony to the man and to the community in which he lives.

My advice to man is this: if it's not broke, don't fix it. Keep your mind clean as much as possible. Don't mess up one of the Spirit of the Universe's most precious and divine designs, which is the human mind. When it comes to alcohol, man needs to find a mindful balance. There is no written history that states drinking wine is a sin. The Bible clearly proves Jesus did not condemn drinking wine any more than he condemned eating bread. However, abuse is sinful. Man has been known to abuse what is not inherently sinful. Eating bread and drinking wine is not sin, but gluttony and drunkenness are. In alcohol use, there is great potential for sin and some potential for profit. In other words, the probability of sin is greater than that of profit.

Your physical organs are the servants of the mind, and your nerves are the messengers that transmit its orders to every part of the body. Anything that lessons your physical power and enfeebles your mind makes it more difficult to discriminate between right and wrong. In other words, over drinking alcohol pushes you off balance, and when you are off balance, you are not where you need to be. As an adult, it is important to know at all times where you are in the moment. When you lose balance, you lose power. When you gain balance, you gain power. A Patriarch should be a balanced man. As a Patriarch, you are the leader of the family and hold the richest title a man can own on this earth. So my man, prove yourself worthy of such ownership.

Man reaches his zenith at the age of sixty; this is the true age of maturity. Sixty is the age of divine. At this stage of life, man must renounce worldliness and generously give back to humanity.

"All things are lawful for me, but all things are not helpful. All things are lawful for me, but I will not be brought under the power of any." (1 Corinthians 6:12)[20]

Woman

: an adult female human being
: all women thought of as a group
: womankind
: distinctively feminine nature: womanliness[1]

A woman is obligated, first and foremost, to love the Spirit of the Universe and then to love herself. She must also come to understand that she was not born for herself alone. A woman's number one desire, outside of love for herself, should be to her husband and their children.

> And the LORD God caused a deep sleep to fall on Adam, and he slept; and He took one of his ribs, and closed up the flesh in its place. Then the rib which the LORD God had taken from man He made into a woman, and He brought her to the man.
> And Adam said:
> "This is now bone of my bones
> And flesh of my flesh;
> She shall be called Woman,
> Because she was taken out of Man."

Therefore a man shall leave his father and mother and
be joined to his wife, and they shall become one flesh.
And they were both naked, the man and his wife, and were
not ashamed. (Genesis 2:21-25)[2]

Sex in marriage is pure and is given for pleasure as well as for
procreation. A woman is uniquely created for the special task of
bearing children. To purposely choose not to have children in order
to pursue other self-centered interests is to forfeit one of the most
rewarding experiences in a woman's life, which is motherhood. The
mother is the heartbeat of the home when loving her husband and
loving and teaching her children. A woman's first duty is to keep
balance in the home.

To the woman He said:
"I will greatly multiply your sorrow and your conception;
In pain you shall bring forth children;
Your desire shall be for your husband,
And he shall rule over you." (Genesis 3:16)[3]

Man and woman were created to build a life together and to balance one another throughout life. Man and woman have vast areas
of individual responsibility, balancing life, shoulder to shoulder as
human beings, equal in humanity.

Motherhood is the most important feminine role a woman can
fulfill. A woman must confirm with her actions that she is a person
of reason, a person of will, a person of great affection, a person
who has a strong desire to achieve the goal of a balanced family,
and she should prove that she has the ability to play her part in this
universe.

"An excellent wife is the crown of her husband, but she who
causes shame is like rottenness in his bones." (Proverbs 12:4)[4]

She opens her mouth with wisdom,
And on her tongue is the law of kindness.

She watches over the ways of her household,
And does not eat the bread of idleness.
Her children rise up and call her blessed;
Her husband also, and he praises her:
"Many daughters have done well,
But you excel them all."
Charm is deceitful and beauty is passing,
But a woman who fears the LORD, she shall be praised.
Give her of the fruit of her hands,
And let her own works praise her in the gates. (Proverbs 31:26-31)[5]

The marital relationship is a delicate balance where each partner, man or woman, makes use of their distinguishing characteristics in order to give the other person what pleases them and what satisfies both of them regarding emotional support and physical needs. To honor and respect your husband does not belittle you, but it does provide some of the discipline needed for a balanced life. The duty of a woman to maintain and take care of a husband is not an easy one. The women who are unaware of this duty may find it difficult to fulfill this responsibility. It is a job for the woman who is aware that this duty requires a great degree of mental discernment and sound judgment.

The older women likewise, that they be reverent in behavior, not slanderers, not given to much wine, teachers of good things - that they admonish the young women to love their husbands, to love their children, to be discreet, chaste, homemakers, good, obedient to their own husbands, that the word of God may not be blasphemed. (Titus 2:3-5)[6]

A wise woman will not believe in love at first sight; such love is a lust that mimics love and is ever so fleeting. Lust is so dangerous that many good lives have come to be ruined because of it. Lasting love is through kindness and permanent affection in the form of a very close friendship.

Before a husband can be your husband, he needs to be your friend. When a friendship turns into the heterosexual relationship of husband and wife, it is the most beautiful graduation this earth has ever known. From the law of duality, with respect to man and woman, comes the principle of increase that is easily seen everywhere in nature. A properly understood marriage symbolizes one of the fundamental laws of life. When two people are willing to strive together and sacrifice for one another, there is a creation of harmony that strikes a balance to which the children of the universe will happily dance. A balanced life is supremely natural and rich.

As a rule of my wisdom, I recommend that a woman should not choose a husband who is under twenty-seven years of age. A man is an adult when he has reached the age of eighteen. Just like it takes a women nine months to give birth to a child, it takes a man nine years to be birthed into manhood. Eighteen years plus nine years equals twenty-seven years. At twenty-seven years of age, all the characteristics of a man, both good and bad, will be more easily detectable, thereby allowing a woman to make an insightful and informed decision when choosing the husband off whom she will reflect (in the same way the moon reflects the light of the sun) as they work together to establish the order of the family. However, after twenty-seven years of life, it will still take another 33 years of life (twenty-seven years plus 33 years equals sixty years) for a human being to reach true maturity. The human being, much like the Joshua tree, reaches true maturity at sixty years of age, for it is at the age of sixty that wisdom is fully enthroned and spirituality blossoms. Sixty is the age of divine.

Once a woman has chosen her man and has made the sacred covenant to be together with him for the rest of her life, she must then forget the past, and the two shall become one. She should not think of any man except her husband, and she should find peace with him. My beloved sisters, if you do otherwise, you will create for yourself one of life's unmanageable conditions and bring harm to your very soul. Never compare your husband to other men. You will achieve nothing by looking at other men and comparing your husband to them, and you will bring yourself to a permanently miserable state.

Once a woman has married, her role as a female changes. A woman must give priority to her husband's needs, even when it is in direct conflict with the needs of her parents, job, or anything else for that matter. Sometimes parents, especially mothers, do not realize that they should leave their daughters alone to allow them to reach an understanding with their own husbands, without parental interference. The most permanent relationship in society is not between parent and child, but between husband and wife. A married couple must always be left alone to plan their own affairs at all levels of life.

The most honorable job for a woman is that of a homemaker. A homemaker can make a home the most pleasant sanctuary on earth for her husband and children. While some women prefer to work at home, other women prefer to work outside the home, sometimes for economic reasons, sometimes for other reasons. Some of the best occupations for women outside the home are nurses, doctors, lawyers, and teachers because these occupations are more agreeable to the female nature. This does not, however, mean that these are the only occupations suited to women.

Women have played many important roles throughout history, and in many cases, have inspired and demanded dramatic change. Today's woman might want to be a journalist keeping people informed of what is going on in their community, a politician who demands change and works to make laws that work for the betterment of everyone, or a community organizer who stands up for civil rights like Rosa Parks and Harriet Tubman. There is a great need in this world for women like First Lady Michelle Obama, Barbara Walters, Oprah Winfrey and Hillary Rodham-Clinton. The empowerment of women is good for all of us. It is perfectly fine for a woman to ask questions and desire wisdom and knowledge just like the Queen of Sheba did with Solomon.

Now when the queen of Sheba heard of the fame of Solomon concerning the name of the LORD, she came to test him with hard questions. She came to Jerusalem with a very great retinue, with camels that bore spices, very much gold, and precious stones; and when she came to Solomon, she spoke with him about all that was in her heart. So Solomon answered all her questions; there was nothing so difficult for the king that he could not explain it to her. And when the queen of Sheba had seen all the wisdom of Solomon, the house that he had built, the food on his table, the seating of his servants, the service of his waiters and their apparel, his cupbearers, and his entryway by which he went up to the house of the LORD, there was no more spirit in her. Then she said to the king: "It was a true report which I heard in my own land about your words and your wisdom. However I did not believe the words until I came and saw with my own eyes; and indeed the half was not told me. Your wisdom and prosperity exceed the fame of which I heard. Happy are your men and happy are these your servants, who stand continually before you and hear your wisdom! Blessed be the LORD your God, who delighted in you, setting you on the throne of Israel! Because the LORD has loved Israel forever, therefore He made you king, to do justice and righteousness." (1 Kings 10:1-9)[7]

Women should have the same basic rights as men and if a woman wants to rule a country, let her study and work hard to show herself approved. A look back at ancient Egypt shows where women were ahead of their time. One of the first women to hold the rank as pharaoh was Hatshepsut. Queen Nefertiti was another Egyptian ruler. She married Amenhotep IV, who preached the belief in only one God. The Egyptian goddess Isis was known originally as the goddess of motherhood and fertility. One of the most famous Egypt's female leaders was Cleopatra. She spoke several languages, studied astronomy and became queen of Egypt at age eighteen. Julius Caesar, the leader of the powerful Roman Republic, and Cleopatra developed a relationship. At that time, Cleopatra had been banished from Egypt by her jealous brother, and Caesar helped her reclaim the throne. The two had a son named Caesarion. Their relationship ended when rival Roman rulers murdered Caesar in the Rome Senate. When Marc Antony became the leader of Rome, he too, developed a relationship with Cleopatra. They had two children and together ruled the most powerful empires in the Mediterranean. Although Hatshepsut, Nefertiti, Isis, and Cleopatra were elite Egyptian women, and the majority of Egyptian women were the most liberated females of their time, a woman's role as wife and mother still came first in the Egyptian society.[8]

A wife should also be a nurse to her husband. In times of illness, a nurse can help a sick person back to health with tender loving care. A husband is much like a small child who needs motherly love in a time of adjustment. In so many ways, the wife takes on the dual roles of wife and mother to her husband.

A wise wife will remain silent during her husband's times of unbalanced anger. It will do the family no good to have two people shouting with anger in the house. There is only one head of the house, not two; anything with two heads is a freak.

A woman should not react sharply to the head of the house, to do so will divide a house against itself. A divided house will eventually lead to fighting, divorce and the break-up of the family. Given enough time, a true man will calm down and regret his unbalanced anger. Eventually, the man will apologize, and after a short time, the family atmosphere will return to balance.

For a woman to be a successful wife, she must win over her husband's heart and be a source of comfort to him. A wife should encourage her husband to do good deeds while persuading him from bad deeds. A wife should not permit her husband to lose interest in her and become interested in other women. If a husband becomes interested in other women, it is either because of his lack of courage or because of her ignorance towards the manifestations of attraction, love, and sex.

The woman has been endowed with the extraordinary power of

persuasion from the Spirit of the Universe, and she should direct that power of persuasion by first making sure that her husband stays interested in her, and then by taking adequate measures to help him maintain his health, to help him be a proper guardian for his family and a good father that their children can respect.

Marriage is a natural necessity for most human beings. Through marriage, the procreation of humanity is continued. A woman should have a partner for satisfying her sexual needs. The natural desire for sex is both strong and necessary, and a woman should have a husband to satisfy her sexual needs in a safe and secure environment.

A woman who is not married resembles a bird without a nest, and marriage can and should serve as a nest for a woman who, without her nest, may feel lost in the wilderness of life. Most of today's social problems are a direct consequence of the lack of a solid family structure.

A family is produced through marriage. Fruit doesn't fall that far from the tree. A child is the fruit of marriage. A good child is most likely to be produced from a good family. The existence of a child is the fruit of the marital tree and a natural desire of a woman. A child strengthens the love between a husband and a wife and serves as the drive for both parents to work together for a better life.

A woman should never underestimate the importance of marriage and motherhood. Both are to her benefit and well-being and the well-being of society as a whole, since they are an integral part of being balanced. Unbalanced people produce an unbalanced society.

The woman represents the Moon. The changing Moon is associated with the woman because its regular twenty-eight-day cycle so closely matches the woman's cycle of menstruation. Just as man represents the Sun, the woman represents the Moon. Like a mirror that reflects the light of the Sun, the Moon represents the shadow side of the Sun's light. A wife is the reflection of her husband and shines brightly from the light reflecting off the sun.

A woman must learn how to be a woman from another woman. Just like iron sharpens iron, so too, is the case with women. A woman must come to understand the 3 stages of her life, how to be a daughter, how to be a wife, and how to be a mother, because this wisdom must be passed on to the next generation, and it is by this wisdom that her womanhood (Queendom) will be established.

The importance of a woman's role as a wife and mother cannot be overstated. In fact, the wisest women of the world, are those women who have enough experience as a wife and mother. A great woman ages gracefully; she doesn't look to chase her youth, but she does look youthful. The father and mother are real partners in the task of raising a child, and although I regard motherhood as sacred, I do not hold a woman solely responsible for the raising of a child.

Motherhood and fatherhood work together as a balancing act that requires both parents to help each other and work together to achieve that balance. Each parent must bring to the family the kind of connection that relates the child to each one of the parents by having a balanced role in developing and enlightening the child's personality on all levels.

A child is first connected to the mother is via the amniotic fluid they share. Amniotic fluid, which surrounds a developing fetus, is flavored by the food the mother eats but it can also be poisoned by alcohol and drug use. It is important that a woman not only watches what she consumes during pregnancy, but also that she controls her stress level.

The mother's role in a child life is second only to the Spirit of the Universe. While the mother provides the child with the inner sense of security for the child's psychological needs, the father looks after the child's external matters, supplying the child with a deep sense of strength and awareness that is required to survive in the outside world.

A man and woman as partners is a relationship that, many times, is founded initially on physical attraction and sex. Such a foundation is unbalanced, fleeting and prone to failure. The foundation of marriage should be based on shared values, not on instant physical attraction. True love is the highest degree of understanding, and when it's between a husband and wife, a higher purpose is present, which leads to having children.

Marriage should be like a strong brick house with love and children acting as the mortar that lies between the bricks, holding the bricks together, and giving strength to the structure. Having children within such a marriage will bring everlasting love, even in times of tribulation. As a husband and wife go through the days of their lives, there undoubtedly will be some very dark nights. However, the children that they produce will twinkle like little stars, reminding them of how bright even the darkest night can be when the stars can be seen.

Child

: an unborn or recently born person
: a young person, especially between infancy and youth
: a son or daughter
: an adult who acts like a child: a childlike or childish person[1]

The family is made up of 3 entities: the man, the woman, and the child. Remove any one of the 3 entities (or sides of a triangle), and the triangle falls apart, which, by the way, is something I view as highly inadvisable. Think about it – do you really want to live in a world of only two dimensions?

Children represent the stars. The universe is not complete without the sun, moon, and stars. Likewise, the family is not complete without man, woman, and child.

The most profound lesson you can ever teach your child is how to connect with the Spirit of the Universe. A child that does not learn how to connect to the Spirit of the Universe will live a life of strain and struggle. There are so many things to teach your child: how to get up when they fall down, how to behave, how to compete, and how to survive in this world are just a few of these lessons. All this is done with one goal in mind, and that is for the child to become mature as an adult. However, the key to maturity as an adult is to know how to balance oneself, and spirituality is very much a part of that balance.

As human beings, we have 3 entities that we need to balance: spirit, soul, and body. Connecting with the Spirit of the Universe allows the child to learn how to achieve that much-needed balance to become a mature adult in his or her life. Figuratively speaking, a person should never stop being a humble child, because a humble child will always look to either his or her father, mother or the Spirit of the Universe for the proper guidance.

> And these words which I command you today shall be in your heart. You shall teach them diligently to your children, and shall talk of them when you sit in your house, when you walk by the way, when you lie down, and when you rise up. You shall bind them as a sign on your hand, and they shall be as frontlets between your eyes. You shall write them on the doorposts of your house and on your gates. (Deuteronomy 6:6-9)[2]

> Children, obey your parents in the Lord, for this is right. "Honor your father and mother," which is the first commandment with promise: "that it may be well with you and you may live long on the earth." And you, fathers, do not provoke your children to wrath, but bring them up in the training and admonition of the Lord. (Ephesians 6:1-4)[3]

Many people assume that success is essentially measured by the amount of money and the things that a person has. While having money and things is necessary and is the creation of someone's success, this type of success will by no means lead to a balanced life on its own, and a balanced life is required to be rich.

The rich life that we want our children to have is a life that is not only measured in money and things, but also in the ability to love and to have empathy, to feel joy, to give charity to those in need, and to know that everyone has a great purpose in life that they must come to know and fulfill in order to be rich.

It is the Spirit of the Universe's divine plan for every human being to enjoy a rich life. The best thing an adult can do for the future of the world is to love and guide a child, and the worst thing an adult can do to the future of the world is to abuse and misguide a child. An abused child left uncured is a future weapon of mass destruction.

Frederick Douglass summed it up well in 1855 when he wrote in a letter stating that "It is easier to build strong children than to repair broken men."[4]

Physical punishment of a child is recommended in the Old Testament, and most of these quotations advocating physical punishment of children appear in the Bible's Book of Proverbs.

"He who spares his rod hates his son, but he who loves him disciplines him promptly." (Proverbs 13:24)[5]

"Foolishness is bound up in the heart of a child; the rod of correction will drive it far from him." (Proverbs 22:15)[6]

"Do not withhold correction from a child, for if you beat him with a rod, he will not die." (Proverbs 23:13)[7]

"You shall beat him with a rod, and deliver his soul from hell." (Proverbs 23:14)[8]

The above quotations in Proverbs describe Solomon's own parenting style when he raised his son Rehoboam, and the following quotations from the Bible's book of first Kings record the negative effects that this parenting style had on Solomon's son. As an adult, Rehoboam was vicious and inconsiderate, with no regard for human rights and no respect for humanity.

Then the king answered the people roughly, and rejected the advice which the elders had given him; and he spoke to them according to the advice of the young men, saying, "My father made your yoke heavy, but I will add to your yoke; my father chastised you with whips, but I will chastise you with scourges!" (1 Kings 12:13-14)[9]

Then King Rehoboam consulted the elders who stood before his father Solomon while he still lived, saying, "How do you advise me to answer these people?" And they spoke to him, saying, "If you are kind to these people, and please them, and speak good words to them, they will be your servants forever." But he rejected the advice which the elders had given him, and consulted the young men who had grown up with him, who stood before him. And he said to them, "What advice do you give? How should we answer this people who have spoken to me, saying, 'Lighten the yoke which your father put on us'?" Then the young men who had grown up with him spoke to him, saying, "Thus you should speak to the people who have spoken to you, saying, 'Your father made our yoke heavy, but you make it lighter on us'—thus you shall say to them: 'My little finger shall be thicker than my father's waist! And now, whereas my father put a heavy yoke on you, I will add to your yoke; my father chastised you with whips, but I will chastise you with scourges!'" (2 Chronicles 10:6-11)[10]

I believe that if a child is abused (this includes physical spanking) then there is a good chance that he or she will engage in anti-social or even criminal behavior as an adult. We, as parents, do not know what level of physical punishment will push a child over the edge and make them become violent and aggressive as adults, which leads me to conclude that, as parents, we should stay away from physical spanking as much as possible.

The universe is in each and every spiritual human being that resides on this earth. A child that is raised with spiritual awareness will learn to understand the basic order and balance that is required to be rich. As parents, we must understand that our children will learn much more from what we do than from what we say. It is up to the parent to allow their spiritual light to shine in words as well as in deeds. By always expressing the spiritual power that exists within you, the child will come to understand their own inner spiritual power. When a person understands the spiritual power that exists within them, they come to realize they are never truly alone. It's impossible to be lonely when you are connected to the whole universe. A spiritually aware person may be alone, but they will never be lonely.

As parents, it is our responsibility to be a role model to our children, to show them how to live a life of character by being accountable for their words and actions. No child can change the genetic cards they were dealt. All children are born to have genetic strengths and weaknesses, predispositions and tendencies. However, we must teach our children that the choices they make can actually affect the expression of those genes, which means we are not exclusively controlled by our genetic makeup. This is how you move out of victimhood and into mastery.

Do not spoil your child. Your child does not have to show you love every minute of every day. The child must accept when the parent says "no," "not now," or "I've got something better." Your child will get over disappointment; it is only a feeling, but it will be hard to get over the feeling of being spoiled. The child must learn to earn what they need and what they value. We must not over-indulge our child with assistance. The child must value independence. We must also allow our child to experience risks.

Play is often considered the opposite of work, but for a child, play is work. Play is the work of childhood. So let the child go outside and play and experience the ups and downs in the world of play - skinned knees, bumped heads, and bleeding scrapes - so they can learn that there will be many falls in life. The key to stopping a fall is in catching yourself in the slip or the trip. Then when the child is a teen, we must share our past mistakes. Experience is the best teacher. However, it's better to let someone else experience the mistake so that you learn from it.

Without children, tomorrow would not be worth the wait, today would not have joy, and yesterday would not be worth remembering. Until you have counted little toes, counted little fingers, held a little hand, kissed a little face, read to little ears, wiped away little tears and cleaned a little booty, you only know a little bit about love.

However, that certainly doesn't mean that every man and every woman must produce a child in order to fulfill their life's purpose.

Bringing a child into this world should be by choice, not by chance. Once the child is in the world, there is no perfect way to be a perfect parent. Each situation is unique. Each parent has different challenges, different skills and abilities, and certainly different children, but what matters most is that you love your child unconditionally. As tenants of this earth, it is the parent's job to keep the child in order, and that order is a balance that starts with the family. There is nothing on this earth that is more bright and more hopeful than a child.

Water

: the clear liquid that has no color, taste, or smell, that falls from
    clouds as rain, that forms streams, lakes, and seas, and that
    is used for drinking, washing, etc.
: an area of water (such as a lake, river, or ocean)[1]

One of the reasons why most sober-minded people find water
so refreshing is because we begin our lives surrounded by water
(amniotic fluid) and therefore, this basic and natural familiarity stays
with us throughout our entire life. The human body is comprised
primarily of water. A 3-day old baby is about ninety-seven percent
water. At about eight months, the baby is about eighty-one percent
water. By the time a human reaches adulthood, the adult body is
still about fifty to sixty percent water, depending on the amount of
fatty tissue and a person's gender.[2]

"Jesus answered, 'Most assuredly, I say to you, unless one is born
of water and the Spirit, he cannot enter the kingdom of God.'"
(John 3:5)[3]

Drinking water helps maintain the balance of body fluids. The
functions of these bodily fluids include digestion, absorption,
circulation, creation of saliva, transportation of nutrients, and the

maintenance of body temperature. The right amount of water will help your heart pump your blood effectively. Most experts recommend that we drink at least nine eight-ounce glasses of water a day, although that is a general guideline. New research is showing that a better determination of how much water a person needs is to drink half of their body weight in ounces of water per day, up to a maximum of 100 ounces.

Remember that the recommended amount of water doesn't take into account your increased need for water after exercise, so make sure to drink more water when you do exercise. A good indicator of how hydrated you are is your urine. When you are properly hydrated, your urine should be clear or very light yellow and should have no odor.

About seventy to eighty percent of your brain tissue is water.[2] When you are dehydrated, both your mind and your body will suffer. When the human body is low on fluids, the brain triggers the body's thirst cues. You must listen to your cues, and get yourself some water, juice or milk - anything but alcohol. Alcohol is not your best choice partly because it is a diuretic, but also because it confuses communication between your brain and your kidneys, causing your body to eliminate more fluids than necessary, which can lead to further dehydration. Although coffee and tea are also considered to be diuretic in nature, if there is no water, juice or milk available, these may be your next best choice.[4]

Water also helps your kidneys. When you are sufficiently hydrated, your kidneys are able to do their very important job of removing toxins from your body through your urine. The reason the odor and color of your urine is a good indicator of your hydration level is that when you are not properly hydrated, your kidneys pull water from your urine to allow other processes in the body to work properly. This, in turn, increases the concentration, color, and odor of your urine.[5]

In fact, if you drink too little water, you will be at risk for kidney stones. Water dilutes the salts and minerals in your urine that form the crystals known as kidney stones and helps keep a healthy balance between the water, salts, and minerals. Kidney stones can form when this balance is thrown off, so drinking plenty of water is a great way to help kidney stones from forming in the first place.

Along with fiber, water is important for good digestion. Water helps your body maintain normal bowel function, and proper hydration keeps things flowing along your gastrointestinal tract. When you don't get enough water, the colon pulls water from the stools to maintain hydration which often results in constipation.[5]

When it comes to your muscles, water is very important. Water helps energize your muscles. When muscle cells don't maintain their balance of fluids, muscles can become fatigued and muscle cramps can occur. Drinking water, especially during exercise, not only helps prevent muscle cramping but also lubricates joints in the body.[6]

Water helps to keep your skin looking good. Dehydration can make your skin look wrinkled and dry. Fine lines and wrinkles appear deeper and more pronounced when you are dehydrated. Your skin's appearance can be improved with proper hydration. Water flushes out impurities, improves circulation and blood flow, and supports cell structure, helping your skin glow. Water is nature's own beauty cream.[6]

Drinking adequate amounts of water is not as difficult as you may think. When paired with slices of fruit or vegetables, served on ice and presented in festive or fancy drinking glasses or pitchers, water becomes an easy, healthy beverage option for any type of party. So take the time to make a habit out of being sober-minded and enjoying the pureness of water. I guarantee your body will thank you for many years to come.

Let it rain, let it rain, let it rain. There are many wonderful and free health benefits brought on by the water that falls from the clouds, also known as rain. Our body needs the rain for the benefits it provides, including those from negative ions. Negative ions are a good thing; they have a net positive effect on your health. There are both positive and negative ions, but as you will see, their names are misleading.

What are negative and positive ions? Ions are all around you right now, and there is a good chance they are affecting the way you feel. An ion is a molecule that has an electrical charge, either positive or negative, that results in the number of protons and the number of electrons not being the same.

Negative ions are created by sunlight, moving air or water, and occur when a molecule gains one or more negatively charged electrons. This causes negative ions to be magnetically attracted to airborne particles such as dust, various pollutants, and potential allergens. The negative ions attach to the dust, pollutants, and allergens, and when enough of them have joined together, they become too heavy to remain floating and fall to the nearest surface. They can then be vacuumed or swept up and removed from your environment, helping to reduce pollutants in the air. Many of the pollutants found in the air reside on floating dust particles, including bacteria and viruses, and may be greatly reduced by the presence of negative ions.[7]

Negative ions are invisible, odorless, and tasteless, and can be found in environments that contain moving water, such as rain, waterfalls, the ocean, the dew, the mist in the mountains, even the shower. The air circulating around moving water contains tens of thousands of negative ions, which explains the amazing feeling you get while taking a walk on the beach, in addition to the natural beauty, of course.[8]

Pierce J. Howard, Ph.D. is the director of research at the Center for Applied Cognitive Sciences in Charlotte, N.C. as well as the author of *The Owner's Manual for the Brain: Everyday Applications from Mind Brain Research*. Dr. Howard says that once the negative ions reach our bloodstream, the ions are believed to produce biochemical reactions. These reactions help relieve stress and alleviate depression. Negative ions increase the flow of oxygen to the brain, which results in more mental energy, higher alertness and decreased drowsiness.[9]

Positive ions are molecules that have lost an electron, also known as positively charged ions, and they have been shown to have a negative effect on our health when we are exposed to them in large quantities. Urban areas typically have a much lower concentration of negative ions in the air than rural areas, and a much higher concentration of positive ions, partially due to all the electronic devices we use on a regular basis. Indoor environments, such as our homes and work places with all their electronic equipment and devices, have an especially high concentration of positive ions, and when our environment contains an excess of positive ions, we often experience tension, anxiety, and irritability, as well as an increase in asthma and allergies.[10]

Water is involved in so many of our bodily functions, including digestion, elimination, and respiration. Water also helps in maintaining safe body temperature and promoting balance within the body, also called homeostasis. Water circulates through the land just as it does through the human body, transporting, dissolving, and replenishing nutrients and organic matter, all while carrying away waste material.

It is a known fact that more than two-thirds of the planet earth is covered by water, yet over six-hundred sixty million people suffer from lack of clean water around the world. This means that a population of people on this planet that is approximately equal to twice the population of the United States does not have access to clean and safe water.[11] Water is by far one of our most vital resources, and when our water is polluted, it is not only devastating to the environment, but also to our health.

Here in the great United States of America, we only need to look at the Flint, Michigan water crises of 2015 (where residents' - including children and the elderly - publicly supplied drinking water was contaminated with lead) to realize we need not take for granted the importance of unpolluted drinking water. The majority of citizens of Flint are either Black, poor, or both, which led me to think: "environmental injustice." Flint is just one example of contaminated city water, but there are many places in this world that are much worse. The quality of our water is directly linked to the quality of our lives and is literally a requirement for staying alive. The general consensus among experts is that an individual can only live for 3 days without water.

Then God said, "Let the waters abound with an abundance of living creatures, and let birds fly above the earth across the face of the firmament of the heavens." So God created great sea creatures and every living thing that moves, with which the waters abounded, according to their kind, and every winged bird according to its kind. And God saw that it was good. And God blessed them, saying, "Be fruitful and multiply, and fill the waters in the seas, and let birds multiply on the earth." (Genesis 1:20-22)[12]

The Bible and water both speak to the Spirit of the Universe's word.

For as the rain comes down,
And the snow from heaven,
And do not return there,
But water the earth,
And make it bring forth and bud,
That it may give seed to the sower
And bread to the eater,
So shall My word be that goes forth from My mouth;
It shall not return to Me void,
But it shall accomplish what I please,
And it shall prosper in the thing for which I sent it. (Isaiah 55:10-11)[13]

Let us know,
Let us pursue the knowledge of the LORD.
His going forth is established as the morning;
He will come to us like the rain,
Like the latter and former rain to the earth. (Hosea 6:3)[14]

"But let justice run down like water, and righteousness like a mighty stream." (Amos 5:24)[15]

The Apostle Paul described the teaching ministry as watering.

Who then is Paul, and who is Apollos, but ministers through whom you believed, as the Lord gave to each one? I planted, Apollos watered, but God gave the increase. So then neither he who plants is anything, nor he who waters, but God who gives the increase. Now he who plants and he who waters are one, and each one will receive his own reward according to his own labor. (1 Corinthians 3:5-8)[16]

The Bible also speaks of purification and cleansing by water.

Then I will sprinkle clean water on you, and you shall be clean; I will cleanse you from all your filthiness and from all your idols. I will give you a new heart and put a new spirit within you; I will take the heart of stone out of your flesh and give you a heart of flesh. I will put My Spirit within you and cause you to walk in My statutes, and you will keep My judgments and do them. (Ezekiel 36:25-27)[17]

"Let us draw near with a true heart in full assurance of faith, having our hearts sprinkled from an evil conscience and our bodies washed with pure water." (Hebrew 10:22)[18]

Water is our lifeline that feeds us and washes us. Water is a gift from the Spirit of the Universe. Water rains down from the clouds and becomes the major driving force on our planet. Like change, water is constant, evaporating into the atmosphere from the oceans, lakes, rivers, and streams. And when the atmosphere can no longer support the moisture within the clouds, we experience rain, snow, hail or sleet. Water provides the earth with the capacity of supporting life, and because of that fact, we must respect water and not take it for granted. Water is a powerful force that has the ability to rot wood and to rust iron. Too much water is destructive, while the right balance cultivates life. The Spirit of the Universe brings beneficial rain which falls at the right time to nourish our crops and to fill our reservoirs.

Having clean water in your life is a luxury that should not be taken for granted because it is a blessing, and is one of the twenty-seven manifestations of balance that is required in order to be rich.

Air

: the invisible mixture of gases (such as nitrogen and oxygen) that surrounds the Earth and that people and animals breathe
: the space or sky that is filled with air[1]

Why is clean air important? The answer to that question seems so obvious that no logical person should ever ask the question in the first place. Every breath we take throughout our days living on earth is done so often and so effortlessly that most of us never give the breathing process a second thought, until we're in a situation where we are unable to breathe or where breathing becomes difficult. If there is too little oxygen in the air, we suffocate. In the hierarchy of needs within the human body, breath is number one. We can go without food for a few weeks and water for a few days, but to be without air for even a few minutes is cause for death. There is a rule of thumb for this concept often referred to as the Survival Rule of 3's, which says that the average person can only survive 3 minutes without breathing air, 3 days without drinking water, and 3 weeks without eating food.

"The Spirit of God has made me, and the breath of the Almighty gives me life." (Job 33:4)[2]

"You hide Your face, they are troubled; You take away their breath, they die and return to their dust." (Psalm 104:29)[3]

Breathing is an unusual bodily function in that it is both involuntary and voluntary. There is only one way for us all to die and that is on an exhale. Breathing is managed in the unconscious, but at any moment we can take control and consciously change how we breathe. This is unlike our other major bodily functions, such as digestion and blood flow, which occur without any sort of conscious influence at all. We can make our breathing fast or slow, deep or shallow, or we can stop breathing altogether by holding our breath.

We breathe to live, but it is also important to learn how to breathe for good health. Breathing exercises can benefit both your body and your mind. It is possible to change our breathing techniques much in the same way that we can change our diet and lifestyle. Focusing on your breathing can have a significant impact on balancing your mind and body while also lowering your blood pressure and helping to reduce anxiety and stress.

Usually, when we think of air and breathing, we think about our lungs rather than the other organs that are also affected by the air we breathe. Let's take a look at what I consider to be 3 of the most important organs in the human body, the heart, brain and lungs, and how air and breathing can influence the function of each of these organs.

In my opinion, the most important organ of the human body is the heart; it is the engine of life. Without the heart, human survival is impossible. The heart is about the size of a closed fist and acts like a pump circulating blood throughout the body. As the blood moves through the lungs, it picks up oxygen and then transports the oxygen throughout the body to the various organs, muscles, and other tissues that need oxygen to function properly. Without the oxygen in the air we breathe, our heart would not be able to do its job.

According to the American Heart Association, tiny pollution particles in the air can lead to big problems for your heart, whether you live in an urban area or a more rural area. Pollution can come from a variety of sources, including traffic, factories, wildfires, and cigarette smoke. Pollution particles related to fuel combustion are a major concern because they are so tiny and can easily enter the human body, irritating the lungs and the blood vessels around the heart. Pollution is believed to have an inflammatory effect on the heart and is also considered to be a contributing cause of chronic inflammation (which, simply put, is the long term over reaction of your immune system). Chronic inflammation is considered to be a contributing factor in cardiovascular illnesses.[4] This is why exercise (which helps the body eliminate toxins, thus reducing inflammation) and a healthy diet (eating anti-inflammatory foods helps the body reduce inflammation) are so important for overall health.

The master of all the actions (both voluntary and involuntary) and all the organs in the human body is the brain. The average adult human brain has about one hundred billion cells. The human brain is the command center for the human nervous system. The five senses of sight, hearing, smell, taste, and touch enable us to have perception of and interaction with our external environment. Disruption of any of the five senses, in my opinion, can trigger a form of disability.

We already know that pollution contributes to inflammation in the body. What is also important is how the brain reacts to inflammation. There is strong scientific evidence suggesting that air pollution changes brain chemistry in a damaging and lasting way. The damage may not be immediate or occur overnight, but with long-term exposure, it can occur. Over the last decade, researchers are learning about how high levels of air pollution may damage children's cognitive abilities and contribute to adult's cognitive decline.[5]

Researchers are also learning about the role that chronic inflammatory reactions play in diseases such as Alzheimer's, Dementia, and Parkinson's. This includes low level chronic inflammatory reactions that result from exposure to air pollutants. That being said, researchers are also quick to point out that the onset of such diseases cannot be attributed to only one factor, but rather, it is the exposure of many factors over the course of one's lifetime that bring about such diseases.[6]

The last, but not least, of the 3 most important organs of the human body is the lungs. The lungs are the most important part of our respiratory system. Our lungs are like air bags, expanding as we breathe in and contracting as we breathe out.

Thus says God the LORD,
Who created the heavens and stretched them out,
Who spread forth the earth and that which comes from it,
Who gives breath to the people on it,
And spirit to those who walk on it. (Isaiah 42:5)[7]

Air quality greatly influences lung function. Pollution damages our lungs, whether from short term high levels of pollution or long term low levels of pollution, the effects are damaging. Some effects of long term exposure to even low levels of air pollution include development of asthma in children, slower lung development in children, damage to the small airways of the lungs, increased risk of death from cardiovascular disease, increased risk of infant mortality, increased risk of developing diabetes, and possible reproductive harm or cancer.[8] Reducing air pollution improves and promotes lung health.

One way we can help reduce pollution is by protecting our trees and advocating that more trees be planted. There are many, many benefits that trees provide us with including reducing stress, cooling the air, and improving our water quality. Perhaps the greatest benefit that trees provide us with is cleaner air.

Trees filter our air as they absorb odor and pollutant gases by trapping them in their leaves and bark. Trees also absorb and store carbon dioxide (a major contributing factor to climate change) and release oxygen back into our air. Over the span of one year, one acre of mature trees absorbs as much carbon dioxide as your car will produce after it has been driven for 26,000 miles.[9]

According to the US Department of Agriculture, in one year,

one acre of forest will absorb six tons of carbon dioxide and release back into the air four tons of oxygen. That is enough oxygen to provide 18 people with as much oxygen as they will need for an entire year.[10]

In today's industrial world, living in an environment that, for the most part, provides us with decent breathable air is a luxury that is required to be rich. Each breath we take depends on the breath we took just before. Being rich has a lot to do with not taking for granted those things that make you a balanced person. Air that is healthy to breathe is very much a part of a balanced life.

We were born on an inhale, and we will die on an exhale. Our entire life rides between that first inhale we take, and that last exhale we release.

Land

: the solid part of the surface of the Earth and all its natural resources: an area of ground
: an area of the earth's solid surface that is owned by someone
: a country or nation[1]

For the purpose of this section, I consider the ground, the land, and the soil to be one and the same, and the earth, as the whole planet or world. Land surface can be sand, soil or stone. Most of the earth's surface is covered with water, and literally, any part that is not water is land. Earth is believed to be the only planet on which water can exist in liquid form on the surface.

Earth is the only *known* planet (or moon) to have consistent, stable bodies of liquid water on its surface. In our solar system, Earth orbits around the sun in an area called the habitable zone. The temperature, along with an ample amount of atmospheric pressure within this zone, allows water to be liquid for long periods of time.[2]

Liquid water (as opposed to water in gas or solid form) is, of course, essential for life as we know it. It is also interesting to keep in mind that the Bible mentioned the earth is round, well before this was scientifically known. (The earth was thought to be flat by early explorers).

"It is He who sits above the circle of the earth." (Isaiah 40:22)[3]

"In the beginning God created the heavens and the earth." (Genesis 1:1)[4]

"And God called the dry land Earth, and the gathering together of the waters He called Seas. And God saw that it was good." (Genesis 1:10)[5]

"One generation passes away, and another generation comes; But the earth abides forever." (Ecclesiastes 1:4)[6]

It was the Spirit of the Universe that created the perfect order of all matter.

Atoms are the basic units of matter and the defining structure of elements. Atoms are made up of 3 particles: protons, neutrons, and electrons. Protons and neutrons are heavier than electrons and reside in the center of the atom, which is called the nucleus. Electrons are extremely lightweight and exist in a cloud orbiting the nucleus. The electron cloud has a radius ten thousand times greater than the nucleus.[7]

The four elements, which are water, air, earth, and fire, form the basis of all life. Each of the four elements are inherently neutral and cannot be considered good or bad. It is man who applied the labels of good and bad to the various actions and properties of the elements.

The same elements that form the material world can also be found within the characteristics of man. The elements of the earth are like that of man: water, breath (air), body (earth), and blood (fire). In order to dive deeply into studying the elements of the universe, a deep dive is needed, indeed, because it is there that the mystery of all things hides.

Soil is a natural resource on the surface of the earth. Soil represents the entire natural world. Without soil there are no plants, without plants, there is no food, and without food, there is no life for plants, animals or humans. Those who teach you that soil simply means dirt have missed the understanding of life. Soil is much like the human body in that it needs healthy water and air to thrive. Soil is the source of life. Therefore, we must not lose our connection with it, because, without it, there is no life.

> This is the history of the heavens and the earth when they were created, in the day that the LORD God made the earth and the heavens, before any plant of the field was in the earth and before any herb of the field had grown. For the LORD God had not caused it to rain on the earth, and there was no man to till the ground; but a mist went up from the earth and watered the whole face of the ground. And the LORD God formed man of the dust of the ground, and breathed into his nostrils the breath of life; and man became a living being. (Genesis 2:4-7)[8]

"For He knows our frame; He remembers that we are dust." (Psalm 103:14)[9]

The dust of the ground is the rich soil from which the body of man was formed, and the breath of life that was breathed into his nostrils is the Spirit of God. Human beings are an integration of God's spirit and an earthly body.

Man is the image of God, which is spirit. Indeed, image-making is strongly prohibited because of its strong ties to idolatry. We may not make images of the Spirit of the Universe for He has already done so. We are His images. It is humans who were created in His likeness, so the Spirit of the Universe placed humans as a living symbol of Himself on the planet earth to represent His reign. All of the world represents creation and destruction. However, we as human beings are a part of a much grander narrative of creation and destruction.

Spirituality and science will always dance to the beat of mystery because human beings can only see so far into the existence of the

Universe, no matter what tool they choose to use.

The human being is a hybrid of spirit, soul, and body. Human beings are the only creatures of the earth that have a spirit within their body as well as the authority to rule the planet earth, which was given to them by the Spirit of the Universe.

Every human being has elements of the Most High Spirit of the Universe within them, but the difference is, some of us are governed more by that Spirit of the Universe than others. In the physical world, man is god.

"I said, 'You are gods, And all of you are children of the Most High.'" (Psalm 82:6)[10]

"Jesus answered them, 'Is it not written in your law, "I said, 'You are gods'"?'" (John 10:34)[11]

"The heaven, even the heavens, are the LORD'S; but the earth He has given to the children of men." (Psalm 115:16)[12]

"I have made the earth, the man and the beast that are on the ground, by My great power and by My outstretched arm, and have given it to whom it seemed proper to Me." (Jeremiah 27:5)[13]

Since the Spirit of the Universe has provided the earth and the land that sits upon it as a collective endowment for humanity, those who have come to own the land as private property must pay taxes in order to provide for those who walk the land and are in need. Meanwhile, all of mankind must collectively come together for the proper care of the planet earth.

For thus says the LORD,
Who created the heavens,
Who is God,
Who formed the earth and made it,
Who has established it,
Who did not create it in vain,
Who formed it to be inhabited:
"I am the LORD, and there is no other." (Isaiah 45:18)[14]

High-quality soils have the ability to hold a large capacity of water. Plants are like people; they need food, water, and oxygen to survive. Healthy soil yields healthy food and healthy food yields healthy people. High-quality soils allow water and air to infiltrate which allow roots to explore and thus allows the earth to give abundantly.[15]

The Latin word humus means soil. The words human, humanity, and humus all come from the same root word, humus. Humus is a dark-brown or black organic component of soil that is formed when plants and animals decay.[16]

Soil organic matter (SOM) is the part of the soil that is made up of decomposing plant and animal tissue. SOM usually makes up a very small percentage of the soil (not much more than 5%) but is still extremely important to the productivity and quality of the soil. The components of organic matter can be broken into 3 major groups: plant residues and living microbial biomass, active soil organic matter, or detritus, and stable soil organic matter, or humus. Incorporating organic materials into the soil can increase the levels of soil organic matter. This is usually accomplished by adding organic materials such as manure or compost.[17]

The components of soil organic matter (SOM) are often classified in 3 ways; "the living," the "dead," and the "very dead." The first major group of soil organic matter components is the "living" group consisting of living organisms. Living organisms, such as earthworms, insects, bacteria, and fungi, make up about 15% of the total composition of the soil organic matter. Insects rip and shred organic material, such as leaves, into smaller pieces so that the bacteria and fungi can use the organic material as food for themselves. The bacteria and fungi aid in the creation of a healthy soil structure, as well as become food for other living organisms, which then, in turn, excrete vital nutrients back into the soil. This group of SOM also aids in maintaining a healthy water holding capacity within the soil.[18]

The second major group of soil organic matter components, often referred to as the "dead," is comprised of active soil organic matter and is easily decomposed (usually ranging between a few months and a few years). This matter makes up about 15% of the total SOM in soil, and also provides the soil with a variety of essential nutrients, specifically sugars and carbohydrates, that can be used as fuel for the bacteria and fungi living within the soil.[18]

The third major group of soil organic matter components is referred to as "very dead," or humus. This matter is very stable and is not easily decomposed. It can resist decay very well, often lasting hundreds of years. Humus makes up about 70% of the total SOM in soil. Humus is important because it encourages soil fertility, healthy soil structure, soil nutrient holding as well as water holding capacity of the soil.[18]

When the land upon which you live is fertile, it possesses a balance of 3: the living, the dead and the very dead. This is also the way of the human body on planet earth. Those who walk in the Spirit of the Universe are the living, those who are unaware of the Spirit of the Universe are the walking-dead, and those who no longer walk this earth, are the very dead. In the Bible, Jesus talked about the walking-dead in the book of Matthew.

"Then another of His disciples said to Him, 'Lord, let me first go and bury my father.' But Jesus said to him, 'Follow Me, and let the dead bury their own dead.'" (Matthew 8:21-22)[19]

Death follows life as life follows death; everything about life and death is resurrection. Living in a rich land produces adequate physical and biological properties to sustain productivity, maintain environmental quality, and promote human, animal and plant health.

One of the most simple and beneficial exercises a human being can do to promote health is to ocean-beach-walk. By being close to the ocean, or any other moving body of water, and walking barefoot on the land (particularly sand), you create a health promoting triangle.

First, by being in the delicate mist of the ocean waters, not only are you in the midst of the life-creating force of moving water, but because of the highly increased amount of negative ions in the air, the air that you are breathing is cleaner and more beneficial to your overall well-being.

Second, when walking barefoot in the sand, you use more energy than you would moving at the same pace on a hard surface. This allows you to strengthen all the muscles from your feet to your back.

Third, an ocean-beach walk allows you to strengthen your heart, improving circulation and your overall cardiovascular health.

There are also thousands of sensory receptors in each of your feet, so not only are you getting the vitamin D you need from the sun by walking barefoot in the sand, but your mind is in touch with the stimuli coming from your feet, which further helps you to be connected and grounded to the earth from which you came while simultaneously connecting you with the world that is around you.

One of the ways sensory receptors are classified is by their location. There are 3 different locations from which your body processes and responds to various types of stimuli. Exteroceptors are found in or on the surface of the skin and respond to stimuli such as touch, pain, temperature, vision, hearing smell and taste. Interoceptors are associated with the autonomic nervous system and respond to stimuli that occur within the body, such as from internal organs or blood vessels. Proprioceptors respond to stimuli that occur in the skeletal muscles, tendons, ligaments, and joints in order to keep track of body position, movement and balance, as well as the physical condition of these areas.[20]

Although we are witnessing multiple conflicts around our world, those conflicts are not what will bring about our demise. Agriculture is not currently adapting as fast as the climate is changing on us. We must understand that healthy water, air and land create a life promoting triangle. When any one of the 3 points of that triangle becomes unhealthy, it gives birth to unbalance, and unbalance, when it is fully grown, brings forth death.

Work

: a job or activity that you do regularly especially in order to earn money
: the place where you do your job
: the things that you do especially as part of your job
: activity in which one exerts strength or faculties to do or perform something
: sustained physical or mental effort to overcome obstacles and achieve an objective or result
: the labor, task, or duty that is one's accustomed means of livelihood
: a specific task, duty, function, or assignment often being a part or phase of some larger activity[1]

When a person hears the word work, the first thing that comes to mind is the duty that is one's accustomed means of livelihood, in other words, a job. I predict that one-third of the jobs in America today will be replaced by machines by the year 2033. Some will say that R. R. Bennett, Sr. is crying robots in the same way that the boy cried wolf. That may be true, however, even in the story of the boy who cried wolf, the wolf did eventually show up.

The world is going digital more and more every day. The good news for future employees who know how to program and repair the robots, is that a decent paying job should be available. However, the transition period from full-time employment as we know it today, to whatever it is that's coming next, will have its share of growing pains, because overall, technology is eliminating far more jobs than it is creating.

Whether you like technology or not, it is plain to see that we live in a tech driven world. The pace of innovation will only increase with more communication mediums and more challenges to the status quo. Network Marketing is a great way to embrace work and social technology. Everyone should try Network Marketing at least once in their life time because of its low risk/high reward business platform.

Work is the seventh manifestation of human balance as well as a desire that is required to be rich. The number seven (as in the seventh manifestation of balance) resonates with the energies and vibrations of "Collective Consciousness." Energy comes from gratitude and work is a form of worship. When you are thankful, you will have more than enough energy to work. We all must be able to work to feel a sense of self-worth. Work is a part of the foundation of our human existence.

There is a process of work that happens well before the birth of a human can ever occur. Be it a dad driving a garbage truck, a mom who is a homemaker, or a child who is playing, work is essential!

Sperm is a cell produced by the male sexual organs that combines with the female's egg during reproduction.[2] The sperm that eventually became you had lots of work to do right from the very beginning. During sexual intercourse, millions of sperm are released from the male in their quest to find the female's egg, and it is not an easy journey. The mortality rate for sperm is very high, and only a few dozen ever make it to the egg. For the lucky few that get near the egg, only one sperm is blessed to work hard enough to penetrate the egg's outer shell and get inside before the others.

When a person is unable to find work, it is not only an economic disruption but also a psychological and cultural breakdown. Depression, domestic violence, drug abuse, suicide, and murder all become more prevalent when a person is jobless and or has nothing meaningful to do. I tell you, beloved; nothing stops a bullet like a job. Many people may not like their job. However, they dislike doing nothing more, and that is because human beings were created to work. Criminals and lazy people are not born, they are made.

"In all labor there is profit, but idle chatter leads only to poverty." (Proverbs 14:23)[3]

Dr. Martin Luther King Jr. said, "If a man doesn't have a job or an income, he has neither life nor liberty nor the possibility for the pursuit of happiness. He merely exists."[4] Dr. King is referring to our Declaration of Independence where it says, "We hold these truths to be self-evident, that all men are created equal, that they are endowed by their Creator with certain unalienable rights, that among these are life, liberty and the pursuit of happiness."[5] We need work in order to achieve balance and a rich life.

I believe an individual should work their entire life in one capacity or another. That doesn't necessarily mean you have to be on someone's payroll, but the need to stay busy is important and should not be neglected.

Sir Isaac Newton's first law of motion states that a body in motion stays in motion. Senior citizens that stay in the workforce are much more likely to retain their physical abilities. The positive psychological impact on a senior citizen who continues to work is big due to the social networking that occurs when a person comes in contact with different people on a daily basis. Furthermore, the senior citizen that stays in the workforce is much more likely to stay up-to-date with technology, which is also a plus in today's fast moving world.

If a person is blessed enough to understand their purpose in life, then in that purpose they will understand the work that they need to get done, and in that work they will understand who they truly are. Work is inherently good, and therefore, you should be able to view the fruit of your labor as good.

Work requires discipline and lack of work breeds regret. There is pain in discipline, and there is pain in regret, but the pain of discipline weighs less than the pain of regret. It boils down to short term discipline-pain or long term regret-pain. When it comes to your work, examine and assess its quality. You should be able to take pleasure and satisfaction in the outcome of your work when that outcome says "job well done."

"He who is slothful in his work is a brother to him who is a great destroyer." (Proverbs 18:9)[6]

Work always reveals something about the one who is doing the work, be it abilities, character or motivation. The original work mandate means to cultivate and to cultivate means to foster growth and to improve. Just like the woman cultivates the seed that comes from the man, parents' work together on the growth and development of the child with the hope of improving their way of life. Work is a form of worship, therefore, do it as though you were working for the Spirit of the Universe and not for people.

"And whatever you do, do it heartily, as to the Lord and not to men, knowing that from the Lord you will receive the reward of the inheritance; for you serve the Lord Christ." (Colossians 3:23-24)[7]

There are twenty-seven manifestations that need to be balanced. One is not more important than the other. Rather, they all work together to create balance between human spirit, soul, and body. There is, however, one exception, and that is number twenty-seven, sex. Sex is the one manifestation that some gifted humans have the discipline to abstain from and yet remain balanced.

Work is a human desire that propels you towards a rich life. Part of being rich is to be able to eat, drink and find enjoyment from the fruit of your work. Work serves a noble purpose and is done to benefit the worker in their pursuit of happiness. The only time success comes before work is in the dictionary.

Do not be a workaholic. Always take the time to balance your life, because in that balance you will find peace, not only for yourself, but others in the world can also find peace by watching you.

We should strive for one hand full of rest over two hands full of work. Harmony is the balance of the multiples and work is essential to our balance. Just as an apple tree will bear apples, faith in the Spirit of the Universe will produce righteous works. True faith and righteous works go hand-in-hand.

> What does it profit, my brethren, if someone says he has faith but does not have works? Can faith save him? If a brother or sister is naked and destitute of daily food, and one of you says to them, "Depart in peace, be warmed and filled," but you do not give them the things which are needed for the body, what does it profit? Thus also faith by itself, if it does not have works, is dead. But someone will say, "You have faith, and I have works." Show me your faith without your works, and I will show you my faith by my works. You believe that there is one God. You do well. Even the demons believe—and tremble! But do you want to know, O foolish man, that faith without works is dead? Was not Abraham our father justified by works when he offered Isaac his son on the altar? Do you see that faith was working together with his works, and by works faith was made perfect? And the Scripture was fulfilled which says, "Abraham believed God, and it was accounted to him for righteousness." And he was called the friend of God. You see then that a man is justified by works, and not by faith only. Likewise, was not Rahab the harlot also justified by works when she received the messengers and sent them out another way? For as the body without the spirit is dead, so faith without works is dead also. (James 2:14-26)[8]

Your work is going to fill a large part of your life, and the only way to be truly satisfied is to do what you believe is great work. And the only way to do great work is to love what you do. If you haven't found it yet, keep looking. Don't settle. As with all matters of the heart, you'll know when you find it. – Steve Jobs[9]

"It's not about how life treats you, it's about how you treat your life." – R. R. Bennett, Sr.

R & R

REST
: repose, sleep; specifically: a bodily state characterized by minimal functional and metabolic activities
: freedom from activity or labor
: a state of motionlessness or inactivity
: a place for resting or lodging
: peace of mind or spirit[1]

RECREATION
: something people do to relax or have fun: activities done for enjoyment
: refreshment of strength and spirits after work; also: a means of refreshment or diversion: hobby[2]

R & R is about making time to unwind and find enjoyment. Be it watching television, taking up a hobby or laughing with family and friends, R & R is a much-needed manifestation of balance.

While watching television, your body is at rest, but your brain is still working. Watching television is more a form of recreation than rest. True rest is when you let your brain rest. One good way to rest is to let your mind relax by thinking about pleasant imagery, which also allows your body to relax. While you rest, your blood pressure decreases and your heart rate slows down. If you want to become more creative, increase productivity, replenish attention, solidify memories and be more patient, let your brain rest.

> Thus says the LORD:
> "Stand in the ways and see,
> And ask for the old paths, where the good way is,
> And walk in it;
> Then you will find rest for your souls." (Jeremiah 6:16)[3]

When you rest, there is a base level of mental tension that totally evaporates. This needs to happen in order for you to truly refresh yourself. Although the brain is always in a state of considerable activity so that it can regulate many automatic functions in your body, when you are not focusing on a specific mental duty, the mental tension evaporates. Rest is not just idleness; it is as indispensable to the brain as vitamin D is to our body.

> Thus the heavens and the earth, and all the host of them, were finished. And on the seventh day God ended His work which He had done, and He rested on the seventh day from all His work which He had done. Then God blessed the seventh day and sanctified it, because in it He rested from all His work which God had created and made. (Genesis 2:1-3)[4]

The verb rested in the above quotation translates to the word Sabbath, which means rest. Many people assume that the word Sabbath means worship, but that is not the case.

It is important to take the time to rest, to dial down, and to step back to see your accomplishments. In other words, rest is a primary condition for stepping back and seeing your life as a whole.

The Spirit of the Universe rested on the seventh day and was satisfied in His accomplishments. The Spirit of the Universe did not rest because of fatigue since the Spirit of the Universe never faints nor is weary.

> Have you not known?
> Have you not heard?
> The everlasting God, the LORD,
> The Creator of the ends of the earth,
> Neither faints nor is weary.
> His understanding is unsearchable.
> He gives power to the weak,
> And to those who have no might He increases strength.
> (Isaiah 40:28-29)[5]

We also must realize how our brain is mentally working, versus mentally resting, based on the environment we subject it to. Living in Midtown, Manhattan, New York City is like having your brain fire off and bounce around like the metal ball in a pinball machine, with all its neon signs, beeping car horns, strangers and loud chatter. Living in this environment is a direct contrast to living in a suburban town that has a small town community feel to it and is also closer to nature, allowing your brain to freely shift its focus from a friendly conversation to the smell of grass, to the song of a bird, to a child's laughter playing in the neighboring yard.

Consciousness is contagious. We are likely to catch the consciousness of what is around us, be it people, places or things. Given enough time we become susceptible to what I call "environmental vibrations."

Rest must be incorporated into your life. Deep rest, like meditation, when incorporated in your life, not only relieves stress and anxiety but is also the way to a peaceful heart.

"My mouth shall speak wisdom, and the meditation of my heart shall give understanding." (Psalm 49:3)[6]

"Come to Me, all you who labor and are heavy laden, and I will give you rest. Take My yoke upon you and learn from Me, for I am gentle and lowly in heart, and you will find rest for your souls. For My yoke is easy and My burden is light." (Matthew 11:28-30)[7]

If you aren't getting enough rest, you may find yourself stressed out. Chronic stress, if not addressed, can cause a host of bad health issues, including headaches, chest pains, digestive issues, lack of ability to focus, and changes in sexual desire.

R & R in the form of a vacation can have real benefits. Vacations revitalize the spirit, soul, and body by distancing a person from their day-to-day duties. New places and social circles allow your mind to drift from one new experience to the next, which is refreshing for a brain that is accustomed to concentrating on a single task for hours at a time, and all of this can lead to a good night's sleep.

However, even your vacation time must be balanced. Most of the benefits you receive while on vacation will dissipate over time and cease to remain refreshing, much in the same way that over drinking alcohol can go from refreshing and fun to a dry hangover.

Once again, we must understand how important it is to be balanced because balance leads to a rich life. Vacations and having a few drinks with friends is much like a nice shower after a long hot day of work. It is refreshing, but still only a fleeting escape.

Recreation balances nearly all aspect of our personal health, much in the same way that getting the appropriate amount of exercise benefits us. It improves mental health, creates strong bones and muscles, and increases the chances of living longer.

Recreation as exercise can come in a variety of ways and can include activities that range from apple-picking to Zumba. What's most important as you choose your mode of recreation is to be sure that you cover the 3 levels of activity: moderately intense activities, vigorously intense activities, and muscle-strengthening activities.

Not getting enough exercise puts you at increased risk for cardiovascular disease, diabetes, and high blood pressure. It is also important to alternate standing and sitting throughout the day because if you sit or stand for too long, you are more likely to have back pain. It is also important to make sure to move around periodically throughout the day because this helps blood flow.

"I know that nothing is better for them than to rejoice, and to do good in their lives, and also that every man should eat and drink and enjoy the good of all his labor - it is the gift of God." (Ecclesiastes 3:12-13)[8]

R & R is the rest and recreation that you need to balance your life. R & R comes from the fruit of your work. R & R is the eighth manifestation of balance. In balance there is enjoyment.

Sleep

: the natural state of rest during which your eyes are closed and
   you become unconscious
: a period of sleep especially of a particular kind
: the natural periodic suspension of consciousness during which
   the powers of the body are restored - for example: REM
   sleep, slow-wave sleep[1]

Sleep is the most important thing to your health. Sleep is non-negotiable. Our sleep is regulated by a powerful internal drive. Going without sleep will make you feel overwhelmingly sleepy. Sleeping relieves sleepiness and ensures that we obtain the sleep we need. Sleep allows the brain and body to change, repair and organize. Sleep allows an individual to restore their equilibrium, in other words, to balance the body. Without the proper sleep, you will surely be knocked off balance.

There has been a link found between sleep deprivation and some well-known disasters, like the destruction of the space shuttle Challenger and the grounding of the Exxon Valdez.[2] On more of an everyday level, sleep deprivation causes a sufficient amount of automobile accidents in the United States as a result of drowsy driving. Tired people tend to be less productive at work, and they are at a much higher risk of traffic accidents, not to mention other health issues.

Lack of sleep affects the body in multiple ways. This is why it is also important to take power naps when possible. The reason why people are physiologically inclined to a slump shortly after midday is because at this point the brain begins to struggle with wake and sleep. It is a power-nap that will break this brain-struggle. Naps don't make up for a good night's sleep, but they do reset your day. If you want improvements in alertness, creative thinking, memory, perception, motor skills, stamina, accuracy performance, as well as enhancement of your sex life, take a nap.

> A twenty-minute snooze - called a stage two nap - is ideal to enhance motor skills and attention, while sixty to ninety minutes of napping brings Rapid Eye Movement (REM) sleep, which helps make new connections in the brain and can aid in solving creative problems. Set an alarm to make sure you get just the right amount of sleep. (Napping for a length of time between twenty and ninety minutes may also help, but you're more likely to feel groggy afterward.)[3]

Our body is naturally designed to sleep twice a day: a longer period at night and a short period in the early afternoon. A daytime nap can help you recover from burnout or an overload of information.

In the evening when it gets dark, the human body produces more melatonin. Melatonin is a hormone that helps your body regulate your sleep and wake cycles. Sleep can be disrupted by many things. Stimulants such as caffeine, medication, alcohol and recreational drug use can keep you up. Distractions such as the sound and light from electronic equipment can prevent you from having a good night's sleep. This is why it is important that you sleep in a dark environment, with no lights or television, because as the brain senses bright light, it reduces melatonin production (thinking that the sun is rising and it's time for you to wake up).

Melatonin helps you fall asleep and sleep well. Some medical experts recommend taking a melatonin supplement before bed because of the way melatonin helps your body regulate your sleep-wake cycles. When your body is maximizing its deep sleep cycles, it is better able to repair and detoxify, which allows you to feel more rested upon waking. Melatonin is also an antioxidant your body needs to recover that has many other benefits such as immune support, inflammation reduction, improved mental, cardiovascular and gastrointestinal health, reduction in headaches, as well as anti-aging benefits.[4, 5]

We must also remember that there should be a transition period as we ease into sleep. Thirty minutes of downtime is sufficient for most people. I recommend meditation. This is instinctive to those of us who are parents. As a mother or father, you don't just put your baby down to sleep, you create some type of transition to ease the child into sleep. Likewise, this transition period also works well for adults.

Your learning and memory depend on both rest and sleep. A sleep-deprived person cannot focus attention optimally and therefore, cannot learn efficiently. Quantity and quality of sleep have a profound impact on learning and memory. If you don't sleep long enough or well enough, you will have trouble with learning and memory. Sleep itself has a role in the consolidation of memory, which is essential for learning new information. Lack of sleep affects our mood, motivation, judgment, and perception in the same way that alcohol does. In other words, walking around with a lack of sleep is like walking around drunk.

There are 3 types of sleep deprivation: total (no sleep within twenty-four hours), partial (disturbed sleep) and selective (not enough sleep). The best sleep is the deep, restorative sleep the Spirit of the Universe gives, which is peaceful and relaxing.

"I will both lie down in peace, and sleep; For You alone, O LORD, make me dwell in safety." (Psalms 4:8)[6]

After a good night's sleep, your mental and physical energy are at the optimal levels for you to achieve the duties which you have set out to accomplish. The gap between getting enough sleep and getting too little sleep may affect your mood long throughout the day.

Getting enough quality sleep will not grant you immunity from disease. However, there is a link between insufficient sleep and some serious health problems. Getting enough quality sleep can also supplement pain medication because being well rested allows you to cope with pain much better. To make each day a safe and productive one, make sure you take the time to get a good night's sleep because sleep is critical to maintaining your balance.

Necessary

Health

: the condition of being sound in body, mind, or spirit; especially, freedom from physical disease or pain
: the overall condition of someone's body or mind
: the condition or state of something[1]

To be healthy is to be free from illness or injury. Health is better to have than wealth. However, the word health means different things to different people. The words health or healthy can also be used in a non-medical context, for example, "A healthy economy." In short, the word health means wholeness, being whole, or sound.

My son, give attention to my words;
Incline your ear to my sayings.
Do not let them depart from your eyes;
Keep them in the midst of your heart;
For they are life to those who find them,
And health to all their flesh. (Proverbs 4:20-22)[2]

"Beloved, I pray that you may prosper in all things and be in health, just as your soul prospers." (3 John 2)[3]

The World Health Organization (WHO) states the following in the Preamble to their Constitution: "Health is a state of complete physical, mental and social well-being and not merely the absence of disease or infirmity."[4]

For the purpose of this book, we will break down the concept of health into two categories: physical health and mental health. Physical health means good body health and can be divided into two sub-categories: structural health and chemical health. Structural health refers to having sound bones, muscles, and organs, as well as structures and systems within the body that are performing properly. Chemical health refers to having the right balance of nutrients in the body as well as keeping the human body free of toxic chemicals as much as possible.

Cells are the smallest unit of life that can replicate independently. The 3 basic parts of all cells are a cell membrane, a nucleus, and a cytoplasm. Cells are the starting point of life, and all living organisms on earth are comprised of cells.

Our bodies are exposed to chemicals in a variety of ways. Exposure comes from our environment, and we may inhale chemicals, swallow chemicals, or absorb chemicals through our skin. In most cases, our body can break down the chemicals or excrete them effectively enough to avoid a toxic overload on our system. The food that we eat, the liquid that we drink, as well as the drugs that we ingest, whether recreational or prescribed to us by our physician, can also have chemicals that can be harmful to our cells and tissues and cause a host of health problems.

Mental health refers to a person's cognitive and emotional well-being, which is how a person thinks, feels and acts. Mental health is important at every stage of life, from childhood to adolescence to adulthood.

Many factors contribute to our mental health, including biological factors, such as genes or brain chemistry, and life experiences, such as trauma or abuse. All people have the potential for suffering from mental health problems no matter our age, whether we are man or woman, wealthy or poor.

Mental health conditions affect your thinking, your mood, and your behavior. There are many types of mental illness and as more research is being done about these illnesses, and more is being learned about them, categories are shifting. There are types of mental illnesses and mental problems that experts generally consider to be the most common, and for the purpose of this book, these are the ones that I am focusing on. This is not meant to include every type of disorder or illness, but rather to summarize some of these conditions.

Anxiety disorders – disorders that affect the way you think and can be described as feelings of anxiety that are more than temporary, get worse over time and interfere with daily life and activities. People suffering from anxiety disorders have mild to severe symptoms when confronted with their anxiety triggers and often go to great lengths to avoid their triggers altogether. Several examples of anxiety disorders are included below.[5]

- Generalized anxiety disorder – general anxiety about day to day life that takes up many hours each day, results in difficulty concentrating or remembering things, is disruptive to normal day to day functions, and is often accompanied by physical symptoms such as exhaustion, headaches, or nausea.[6]
- Social anxiety disorder – much more than shyness, this disorder results in intense and irrational fear of social humiliation and people who suffer from this type of anxiety disorder will avoid many types of social interactions, such as contributing to group discussions or interacting with peers in conversation.[6]
- Panic disorder – sudden and recurrent periods of intense fear, increased heart rate, choking, shortness of breath, fear of recurring future attacks, avoidance of triggers and places where previous attacks have occurred.[7]
- Phobias – strong and usually irrational fear of something that usually is not dangerous or harmful. There are many specific types, including social phobia, often results in physical symptoms like trembling, elevated heart rate, or difficulty breath-

ing.[8]

- OCD (Obsessive-Compulsive Disorder) – obsessions are distressing repetitive thoughts that occur over and over (such as fear of germs), and compulsions are the behaviors you engage in over and over to combat those upsetting thoughts (washing your hands or cleaning constantly), and can be severe if left untreated.[9]
- PTSD (Post-Traumatic Stress Disorder) – occurs after a traumatic event (such as an accident, war, natural disaster or physical abuse), and consists of feelings of fear and stress that occur after the event is over and the actual danger has passed. Symptoms include flashbacks, difficulty sleeping, nightmares reliving the traumatic event, frequent anger, feelings of depression or anxiety.[10]

Mood disorders – also referred to as affective disorders and result in feelings of chronic sadness, sometimes changing between extreme happiness and extreme sadness. Some examples of mood disorders are included below.

- Depression – variety of causes (such as trauma, genetics, life circumstances, brain structure, medical conditions, or drug and alcohol abuse). Symptoms include changes in sleep patterns and eating habits, lack of energy, difficulty concentrating, low self-esteem, or physical pain. Most patients respond well to treatment, but depression can be detrimental if left untreated.[11]
- Bi-Polar Disorder – no single cause has been identified, but experts agree common causes include stress, genetics, and brain structure. Symptoms include extreme changes in mood from highs (mania) to lows (depression), unpredictable behavior, impaired judgment, difficulty sleeping, oversleeping, and the inability to perform normal tasks due to extreme depression.[12]
- SAD (Seasonal Affective Disorder) – type of depression causing mood changes during winter months when there is less natural sunlight that usually goes away during spring and sum-

mer months when exposure to sunlight increases. Symptoms include irritability, feelings of hopelessness, difficulty sleeping, oversleeping, changes in weight, fatigue, loss of energy, sadness, anxiety, and loss of interest in activities normally enjoyed by the individual.[13]

Some other types of mental illnesses or disorders that I did not mention are Substance Use Disorder, ADD (Attention Deficit Disorder) and ADHD (Attention Deficit Hyperactivity Disorder), eating disorders (such as Anorexia, Bulimia, and Binge Eating), Personality Disorders (such as Antisocial Personality Disorder and Borderline Personality Disorder) and Psychotic Disorders (such as Schizophrenia).

I see health as the state of being sound in spirit, soul, and body, as well the ability to be flexible and adapt to the stresses of life, allowing you to bounce back from adversity while striving to achieve balance. Self-care is at the beginning of health-care. In short, health is the ability to be rich and enjoy life.

Wellness

: the quality or state of being healthy
: the quality or state of being in good health especially as an
      actively sought goal[1]

Wellness is the integration of spirit, soul, and body that allows us to achieve optimal balance as individuals with the explicit goal of making both our homes and our communities better. Wellness is a way for an individual to maximize their potential. Balance and wellness could be defined as one and the same in terms of the purpose for writing this book. Wellness is the lifetime process of working towards enhancing your spiritual, intellectual, emotional and physical well-being. If an individual concentrates on his or her wellness, not only will they reap the rich rewards of wellness, but their family and community will surely reap those rich rewards as well.

"I will praise You, for I am fearfully and wonderfully made; Marvelous are Your works, and that my soul knows very well." (Psalm 139:14)[2]

The World Health Organization defines wellness as the optimal state of health of individuals and groups. There are two focal concerns: the realization of the fullest potential of an individual physically, psychologically, socially, spiritually and economically, and the fulfillment of one's role of expectations in the family, community, place of worship, workplace and other settings.[3]

The National Wellness Institute uses a 3-prong definition for wellness:
- Wellness is a conscious, self-directed and evolving process of achieving full potential
- Wellness is multi-dimensional and holistic, encompassing lifestyle, mental and spiritual well-being, and the environment
- Wellness is positive and affirming[4]

Wellness is more than being free from disease or infirmity, it is a dynamic process of balance, and there are nine classes of wellness that need to be balanced.

1. Spiritual Wellness is the ability to have a relationship with the Spirit of the Universe. This is a resource that is always available to an individual when coping with the everyday issues of life because even the best of people cannot be sufficient help for you when your spirit is grieved. We are all plugged into the spiritual world; we just need to turn ourselves on. Having a relationship with the Spirit of the Universe allows us to be in-tune with ourselves. In spirituality, we will find meaning in life events as well as our own individual purpose. Spirituality allows you to understand creation and destruction and how to appreciate your life experiences for what they are. You will be able to strive towards an order in your life that leads to being balanced and rich.

2. Intellectual Wellness is all about right-thinking: keeping your thoughts logical and reasonable. Think about those things that are true. Think about those things that are honorable. Think about those things that are just. Think about those things that are commendable. Think about those things that are of love, because how you think has everything to do with what you will become.

3. Emotional Wellness refers to understanding your feelings. We must be attentive to both our negative and positive feelings. We must understand how to master both of these emotions because they can play a major part in our decision making. We must understand that the worst emotions among us can be weaponized and used to advance a wrongful agenda. Many bad decisions have been made based solely on how a person was feeling. There are groups of people all over the world who like to tap into anger and fear in order to advance hate. It is very important not to let your emotions supersede your intelligence. Once you have mastered emotional wellness, you will understand yourself better and move towards being more balanced.

4. Physical Wellness is all about maintaining a healthy body and seeking care for that body at the first sign of illness, or whenever else care is needed. It is important to stay conscious of your physical health at all times. Physical wellness is maintained through getting the proper sleep, nutrition, and exercise, and in doing so, you also help to build your sense of self-esteem, self-control, and self-worth.

5. Educational Wellness is all about continuing to expand your knowledge. A person's learning process should begin in the cradle and continue straight through to the casket. A person should always be an active participant in some form of cultural, community or scholastic activities. These activities will expand your knowledge while allowing you to share the knowledge you already have with others. In order to become more knowledgeable and better-rounded as a person, you must be educated in new ideas and understandings. Educational wellness encourages all 3 learning levels of life, which are learning, unlearning and relearning.

6. Financial Wellness involves the process of how you successfully manage your money. There is no way to miss the fact that money plays a critical role in our well-being. In fact, not having enough money is a common source of stress, which means that financial wellness is all about money management. It

is very important that a person makes money but doesn't allow money to make them. Money must be balanced to achieve financial wellness.

7. Occupational Wellness encourages personal satisfaction, balance, and enrichment in one's life through work. There is nothing better than a person feeling or hearing "job well done." Gratitude begets energy. Work is all about having the right attitude regarding labor and how it has been a very important part of our existence from conception. When pursuing a career, think about what your purpose in life is by first deciding what you enjoy doing most. The way to communicate your value and purpose is through occupational activities. Your contributions to the universe rest on your purpose and your love for mankind.

8. Social Wellness is a class of wellness that helps you develop healthy relationships with peers; it is all about how we interact with others. Having a good social network is more valuable than gold at its largest scale. Your network is your net worth. A positive social network will make your net worth positive. It is not what you know as much as it is who you know. The 3 keys to social wellness are listening, learning and assertiveness.

9. Environmental Wellness is living a life style where the environment respects the living and where the living respect the environment. It is important to stay conscious of your environment, which includes anywhere you sleep, work and play. There is an undeniable balance between nature and man that must be achieved for the benefit of all parties involved. Simply put, environmental wellness draws harmony from the interaction of nature and man.

In order to maintain wellness, one must be aware of energy leaks that can occur due to arguments and disagreements, which can lead to depression. When we balance the spiritual, intellectual, emotional, physical, educational, financial, occupational, social and environmental aspects of our life, we achieve a wellness that leads to being balanced and being rich.

Sickness

: unhealthy condition of body or mind
: the state of being sick
: a specific type of disease or illness
: the feeling you have in your stomach when you think you are
    going to vomit
: a disordered, weakened, or unsound condition
: nausea, queasiness[1]

The first thing we must understand about sickness is that no one is free from sickness their entire life. We all get sick one day in one way or another. Sickness and the matter of healing touches every one of us. Some sickness comes because we don't take good care of ourselves, some sickness comes because we abuse ourselves and some sickness comes so that we can experience healing. In this fast-paced world where it takes very little time to get from one side of the world to the other, and which seems to be getting smaller and smaller with each passing day, not only is the Spirit of the Universe important, but doctors and vaccines are also important when we discuss sickness and healing.

All of us know something about the feeling of sickness. It is perfectly fine to appeal to the Spirit of the Universe for healing. However, it is foolish for anyone to suggest that the use of doctors and medicine displays a lack of faith. I believe in the power of the Spirit of the Universe, but I also believe in the power of science and medicine, and whether a believer is healed through medicine or miraculous means, all healing is ultimately from the Spirit of the Universe.

The immune system is the way our bodies fight infectious microorganisms, or antigens, as they enter the body. Antigens are any foreign substances that cause an immune response within the body and include viruses, bacteria, and fungi. The immune system is often referred to as the lymphatic system and is comprised of organs and tissues that work together to fight infections and diseases. The lymphatic system consists of lymph, lymph nodes, lymphatic vessels, white blood cells, spleen, bone marrow, thymus, and tonsils. Lymphatic tissue also exists in the bowel and small intestine. More than half of all cells in the body that produce antibodies can be found in the walls of the bowel, and these cells can recognize and then destroy pathogens in the body. Lymphatic tissue is also present in the mucus membranes where they can destroy pathogens as they enter the body.[2]

- Lymph – a clear fluid that travels through the lymphatic system and carries cells (such as white blood cells) that help fight infections and other diseases.[2]
- Lymph nodes – small bean shaped organs of lymphatic tissue that are surrounded by connective tissue. Lymph nodes filter lymph, store white blood cells, activate the production of specific antibodies, and are connected to one another by lymphatic vessels. When they become painful or swollen, it can be a sign that your body is actively fighting an infection.[2]
- Peyer's patches – lymphoid tissue in the small intestine.[4]
- Lymphatic vessels – a network of thin tubes that carry lymph and white blood cells to the lymphoid organs, branching out like blood vessels into all the tissues of the body.[2,4]
- White blood cells – made by bone marrow and help the body

fight infection and other diseases. There are lots of types of white blood cells.[2]

- Spleen – an organ on the left side of the abdomen, near the stomach, about the size of your fist. It is responsible for storing and removing blood platelets, storing defense cells, and destroying old red blood cells.[2,4]
- Bone Marrow – sponge-like tissue inside your bones where many defense cells are produced and multiply before entering the bloodstream where they can then move to other organs or tissues.[3]
- Thymus – an organ in the chest behind the breastbone that is only fully developed in children. Once we reach adolescence the tissue in this organ begins to turn into fat tissue. T (thymus) lymphocytes are one type of white blood cells and are formed in bone marrow but then move to the thymus where they mature and become T cells.[3]
- Tonsils – 2 masses of soft tissue at the back of each side of the throat (left side and right side) that are comprised of tissue that is similar to the lymph nodes. They provide the first line of defense for the immune system against bacteria or viruses entering your mouth and help to immediately activate the immune system.[3]

Most people look at sickness as always a bad thing, but that is just not true. In sickness you can find balance. In fact, most, if not all cures are developed from the ability to understand sickness.

"Is anyone among you sick? Let him call for the elders of the church, and let them pray over him, anointing him with oil in the name of the Lord. And the prayer of faith will save the sick, and the Lord will raise him up." (James 5:14-15)[5]

Sometimes a period of sickness can balance our minds and allow us to think seriously about the order of our priorities. You may be living your life as if you are not going to ever die, but should you get sick, that sickness can bring death into perspective. Sickness can also prepare us to have empathy for others. Often if a loved one gets sick, we quickly become aware of life and death. Without sickness, you cannot appreciate the work that goes into health, wellness, or the totality of life.

Joy

: a feeling of great happiness
: a source or cause of great happiness
: something or someone that gives joy to someone
: success in doing, finding, or getting something
: the emotion evoked by well-being, success, or good fortune or
    by the prospect of possessing what one desires
: a state of happiness, felicity or bliss
: a source or cause of delight[1]

Joy is the second of the nine attributes of the fruit of the Spirit.

"But the fruit of the Spirit is love, joy, peace, longsuffering, kindness, goodness, faithfulness, gentleness, self-control." (Galatians 5:22-23)[2]

Joy is more than happiness. Having fun can make you happy, but joy is much more than being happy. Happiness is of the soul, what you think and what you feel. Happiness is fleeting and temporary. But joy is of the spirit, which is the center of man and the best part of man. Joy is spiritual. When a man experiences joy, it is a complete feeling, and all aspects of his spirit, soul, and body are wrapped in that joyful bliss.

To miss joy is to miss the goodness of life. A life without joy is a life of waste and greed, constantly pleasure seeking, thinking only of self, with no regard for the laws of nature that require order and balance. A good example of this is Rome and Greece during their decline. They were notorious for their pleasure-seeking culture of festivals which lasted for days and weeks and were often termed orgies. When a man is deprived of spiritual joy, then that man will seek cardinal pleasures. To live a joyful life, you must first understand where to find joy. Joy comes from loving the Spirit of the Universe.

> As the Father loved Me, I also have loved you; abide in My love. If you keep My commandments, you will abide in My love, just as I have kept My Father's commandments and abide in His love. These things I have spoken to you, that my joy may remain in you, and that your joy may be full. (John 15: 9-11)[3]

Joy is an essential spiritual practice that grows out of love. If you show me someone who can't find faith, I'll show you someone who can't find love. You need faith to love and you need love to find joy. Joy is not the product of the natural mind but the product of the supernatural Spirit of the Universe. Since the Spirit of the Universe is the author of all that is considered good, including joy, then to follow the Spirit of the Universe is to have joy follow you.

Joy is a gift from the Spirit of the Universe, so unwrap it, take it out of the box, put it on and be glad to show it off, because joy is evangelistic, missional and mountain moving.

Joy is emotional and you want to share it because it is forever seeking company. Joy is a feeling, and not just a fraction of a feeling, but a complete, full and positive feeling. Depending on the intensity of the feeling, joy can range from the quiet charm of watching your child sleep peacefully at home, to the loud cheer of watching that same child hit a home run for his little league baseball team. Joy is the complete response you feel when the emotion of happiness and the emotion of love start to dance with one another.

Don't seek joy as if it were happiness, which is based on material things and events. We cannot manufacture joy. Seek the supernatural mountain moving power of the Spirit and the Spirit of the Universe will give you joy. This, I tell you, is as certain as gravity is on earth.

Joy is something that is constant because it lives within us and not outside of us. No person and no thing can take your joy. You can have the same joy in terrible circumstances that you have when all is well, as long as you stay in the presence of the Almighty Spirit of the Universe.

The Spirit of the Universe allows for us to experience joy every day. Joy in its truthfulness has a moral dimension, and therefore, is an obligation. If we can't find a reason to be joyful, then our perspective on life must change. Joy isn't like happiness, which is based on what is happening right now. Although joy and happiness can be experienced at the same time, happiness is based on material things and events. Joy is a permanent possession, while happiness is ever so fleeting. Once you are given joy by the Spirit of the Universe, you possess it, own it, and don't have to give it up for anything or anyone, regardless of the circumstances.

> Most assuredly, I say to you that you will weep and lament, but the world will rejoice; and you will be sorrowful, but your sorrow will be turned into joy. A woman, when she is in labor, has sorrow because her hour has come; but as soon as she has given birth to the child, she no longer remembers the anguish, for joy that a human being has been born into the world. Therefore you now have sorrow; but I will see you again and your heart will rejoice, and your joy no one will take from you. And in that day you will ask Me nothing. Most assuredly, I say to you, whatever you ask the Father in My name He will give you. Until now you have asked nothing in My name. Ask, and you will receive, that your joy may be full. (John 16:20-24)[4]

We can "suffer-rejoice." In other words, we can suffer hardship and still understand the bliss of joy that exists. The practice of "suffer-rejoicing" produces spiritual patience and strength. As we work towards mastering spiritual patience and strength, we are completing a task of the Spirit of the Universe, and in doing this, we gain maturity.

> Blessed be the LORD,
> Because He has heard the voice of my supplications!
> The LORD is my strength and my shield;
> My heart trusted in Him, and I am helped;
> Therefore my heart greatly rejoices,
> And with my song I will praise Him. (Psalm 28:6-7)[5]

"You will show me the path of life; in Your presence is fullness of joy; at Your right hand are pleasures forevermore." (Psalm 16:11)[6]

"My brethren, count it all joy when you fall into various trials, knowing that the testing of your faith produces patience. But let patience have its perfect work, that you may be perfect and complete, lacking nothing." (James 1:2-4)[7]

Joy is a complex balance of what we think and how we feel, of love and happiness, of situations and events, and of our actions, that all come together in one big tasty gumbo pot of life. Joy delights in the good that is. Joy is a necessary prong of a rich life. Joy is much richer than any happiness and is often found at the corner of success and significance.

Remember, above all things, never let anything or anyone steal your joy.

"When they go low, we go high." - President Barack and Michelle Obama[8]

Contentment

: the state of being happy and satisfied: the state of being content[1]

Being content is to have all that you need or the ability to find all that you need in life. Contentment is the acceptance of how things are. You need to be both accepting of what is and adaptable towards what is not. In other words, don't try to stop the flow; flow within the flow. Contentment is not complacency. Be content with what you have and patient for what is to come.

Let your conduct be without covetousness; be content with such things as you have. For He Himself has said, "I will never leave you nor forsake you." So we may boldly say: "The Lord is my helper; I will not fear. What can man do to me?" (Hebrew 13:5-6)[2]

Take pride in your adulthood. There is a dual meaning to "a rolling stone gathers no moss." You must understand it's important to be still for some time in order for you to take root. There is no fruit without a root. But on the other hand, stagnation prevents growth.

Contentment and growth are partners in life. Never stop growing. No matter your age, your higher-self yearns for growth. The problem is that most people don't know how to satisfy their yearning.

The average American citizen dies in their forties and gets buried in their seventies. Human beings don't grow old and die, they stop growing and die. It is at the age of divine (sixty years old) when a person should have developed enough gratitude to gracefully navigate their remaining days of life before passing through the door of death.

Contentment is individualized. We must create contentment in our own lives. No one can do it for you because creating contentment is about personal strong-holds and adjustments.

Striving for contentment is simple but not easy. It's about working with what is working and stopping what isn't. It is all about balance. Often, it's as simple as cleaning house and taking out the trash, and I mean this figuratively as well as literally. In a very real way, you have to be willing to take out your own trash.

Contentment is a choice. No one knows better than you what you need and what you don't need. You must be truthful with yourself. The truth is, the original you is not bad. The only bad is the bad personal relationship we have with ourselves.

Every human being is good and beautiful in his and her own way, so if you think or feel bad about yourself, then the relationship you have with yourself is bad. Contentment is a beautiful thing, and you will know when you have it because when you do, you'll awake most days with excitement for the new day ahead.

The worst thing you can do in your pursuit of contentment is to believe in the saying "the more, the merrier." Belief in this idea will kill your pursuit of contentment because too much of anything will kill you. When you think contentment, think "I need less." By that, I mean less external pressure and less internal pressure. The key is to learn how to do more with less.

Contentment comes in trusting yourself. You cannot control what happens outside of you. It is a waste of mental, emotional and physical energy to devote your attention to things you cannot change. You have to accept the things you cannot change. But you must also have the courage to change the things that you need to.

However, every fight doesn't deserve a tangle. Sometimes we need to surrender, not as a coward but as an act of humbleness. This reminds me of the Serenity Prayer that is commonly attributed to the American Protestant Theologian Reinhold Niebuhr (1892-1971).

God, grant me the Serenity
To accept the things I cannot change...
Courage to change the things I can,
And Wisdom to know the difference.

Living one day at a time,
Enjoying one moment at a time,
Accepting hardship as the pathway to peace.
Taking, as He did, this sinful world as it is,
Not as I would have it.
Trusting that He will make all things right
if I surrender to His will.
That I may be reasonably happy in this life,
And supremely happy with Him forever in the next.
Amen.[3]

In the Serenity Prayer, I see a 3-fold message that focuses on personal responsibility, discipline, and humility. All 3 traits are needed when striving towards contentment. If you want the world to be a better place, you must become better. Start with yourself. Necessity is the mother of invention. When it becomes imperative that you must reinvent yourself, you must first come to that understanding, and then you make the change.

Discipline is not truly discipline unless you have the freedom to change your path and the freedom to not change your path. In other words, discipline is not truly discipline unless you have the freedom to make your own choice for yourself in that instance.

Likewise, freedom is not true freedom without the proper amount of discipline. Discipline cannot come without freedom and freedom must be disciplined. There is a balance between discipline and freedom that must be mastered.

Many times, curiosity is one of our greatest challenges in life because curiosity is the desire to know something or do something new that may or may not be good for us. But once that something has been acquired, one must be mindful of the desire for more. More is at the threshold of greed, and no amount of possessions will satisfy greed.

Greed will always outrun possessions. Discontent is greed's twin brother and will always raise its ugly head to become an obstacle to contentment. Greed, if allowed to grow, will give way to a habit, and that habit will gain its power through repetition. The more you do it, the stronger it gets. Anything you do as a habit that is not good in nature will become your enemy, and your enemy does not want you to achieve a state of contentment.

"He who loves silver will not be satisfied with silver; nor he who loves abundance, with increase. This also is vanity." (Ecclesiastes 5:10)[4]

You must watch where you place your focus because whatever you focus on will expand. Have you noticed that when you buy a car you start noticing a lot of people driving the same model? That is because you are hypersensitive to that model. If you focus on what is right in your life, then that focus will expand and begin to devour that which is wrong.

Real life is full of disappointments, inconveniences, and losses. If you want to live a rich life, you're going to have to learn how to balance the full range of emotions that come as a result of both setbacks and gains.

Always remember that the Spirit of the Universe is more concerned with your growth than with you being comfortable, and contentment is much about understanding the purpose of being uncomfortable.

"The LORD is near to those who have a broken heart, and saves such as have a contrite spirit." (Psalm 34:18)[5]

"And we know that all things work together for good to those who love God, to those who are the called according to His purpose." (Romans 8:28)[6]

Wealth is the abundance of valuable material possessions. Wealth without balance is artificial richness. In fact, wealth often leads to rejection of the Spirit of the Universe. Part of being rich is being content.

While material possessions play only a small part in living a rich life, that does not mean that poverty is a good thing. I consider true poverty to be the lack of basic material requirements that are necessary for living a decent life that is free from hunger, disease, and exposure to the elements. Much more about food, shelter, and clothing will be covered in the later chapters of this book.

Inner peace is the wisdom needed to balance the multiples in our life. To have inner peace is to be free from anxiety, needs or wants. These 3, anxiety, needs, and wants are the root of suffering.

Contentment is the result of no longer being ruled by the root of suffering. Contentment is understanding that you are exactly where you should be at that exact moment in your life.

Not that I speak in regard to need, for I have learned in whatever state I am, to be content: I know how to be abased, and I know how to abound. Everywhere and in all things I have learned both to be full and to be hungry, both to abound and to suffer need. I can do all things through Christ who strengthens me. (Philippians 4:11-13)[7]

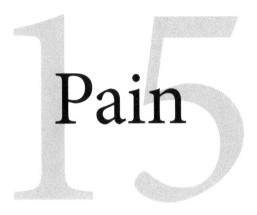

Pain

: punishment
: localized physical suffering associated with bodily disorder (as a disease or an injury)
: a basic bodily sensation induced by a noxious stimulus, received by naked nerve endings, characterized by physical discomfort (as pricking, throbbing, or aching), and typically leading to evasive action
: acute mental or emotional distress or suffering: grief
: the throes of childbirth[1]

Pain is something we all experience at one time or another and it can take on various forms as it moves throughout our lives. In fact, fear is nothing more than anticipated pain, whether it's physical, emotional, mental or spiritual. Human beings have 3 types of pain, physical pain, soul pain and spiritual pain, and all pain is subjective in nature. In other words, what is painful to me may not be painful to you.

Pain is an individual experience. There are many descriptors of physical pain including aching, burning, dull, sharp, or radiating, but generally speaking, physical pain is what most people refer to when they say something hurts on or in their body. However, no matter what kind of pain you have, it will most likely be difficult to quantify because of the subjective nature of pain. Soul pain, which is mental and emotional (psychological) pain, can be described as suffering. As for spiritual pain, I describe it as a person's inability to connect to a source of meaning and hope, and this connection is required for living a balanced life.

All pain can be defined as unpleasant. The sensation of pain can be divided into two categories: primary pain and secondary pain. Primary pain is any unpleasant sensation you feel as a result of illness or injury. Secondary pain is the human agony we feel as a reaction to primary pain. Feelings like anger, jealousy, anxiety, despair, and depression that we allow to grow on top of any unpleasant sensations also fall into the category of secondary pain, but they may not have a physical origin.

When this happens, we become a human land-fill that is bogged down with toxic reactivity. Beloved, don't allow yourself to be bogged down. Dress yourself with the complete set of spiritual armor. There are six pieces of spiritual armor: the belt of truth, the breastplate of righteousness, the boots of peace, the shield of faith, the helmet of salvation and the sword of the Spirit of the Universe. All of these pieces are needed for the spiritual battlefield, so dress-up!

Finally, my brethren, be strong in the Lord and in the power of His might. Put on the whole armor of God, that you may be able to stand against the wiles of the devil. For we do not wrestle against flesh and blood, but against principalities, against powers, against the rulers of the darkness of this age, against spiritual hosts of wickedness in the heavenly places. Therefore take up the whole armor of God, that you may be able to withstand in the evil day, and having done all, to stand. Stand therefore, having girded your waist with truth, having put on the breastplate of righteousness, and having shod your feet with the preparation of the gospel of peace; above all, taking the shield of faith with which you will be able to quench all the fiery darts of the wicked one. And take the helmet of salvation, and the sword of the Spirit, which is the word of God; praying always with all prayer and supplication in the Spirit. (Ephesians 6:10-18)[2]

Most people describe jealousy as a crazy feeling of pain. There is jealousy that is sin and there is jealousy that is righteous. A practical example of righteous jealousy is when a husband gets jealous because another man is flirting with his wife; he has the right to be jealous because only he has the right to flirt with his wife. Likewise, the Spirit of the Universe is jealous when someone gives to another worship and service that belong to Him.

You shall have no other gods before Me. You shall not make for yourself a carved image—any likeness of anything that is in heaven above, or that is in the earth beneath, or that is in the water under the earth; you shall not bow down to them nor serve them. For I, the LORD your God, am a jealous God, visiting the iniquity of the fathers upon the children to the third and fourth generations of those who hate Me, but showing mercy to thousands, to those who love Me and keep My commandments. (Exodus 20:3-6)[3]

Pain can manifest itself in our lives in many ways from alcohol and drug abuse to being overweight. Always investigate the process you define as pain. You must realize that pain is a mass of sensation that has no definite shape. Pain is not a tangible thing. The most important key to modifying pain is awareness. With awareness, we can reduce secondary pain. You need to be aware that pain is a sign of weakness that must be corrected and made strong or else it will overcome you.

And He said to me, "My grace is sufficient for you, for My strength is made perfect in weakness." Therefore most gladly

I will rather boast in my infirmities, that the power of Christ may rest upon me. Therefore I take pleasure in infirmities, in reproaches, in needs, in persecutions, in distresses, for Christ's sake. For when I am weak, then I am strong. (2 Corinthians 12:9-10)[4]

A lot of the world's suffering comes from people who are afraid or unaware of how to deal with their innermost fears. When they take a look at themselves, they become fearful. Remember, fear is nothing more than anticipated pain.

Fear can become so overwhelming that it hurts, and hurt people have the great ability to hurt other people. That's why it is so important to be mindful of your pain and not pass your pain on to others.

Holding on to pain is just as bad as passing it on to others; it is a form of self-punishment and includes drug abuse, domestic violence, murder, and suicide. All of these behaviors are the result of people who are suffering and not dealing with their pain.

Unless you understand pain, you will never overcome it. Pain calls us to pay attention in order to self-evaluate. Pain lets us know we are out of order and off balance and that we are in need of healing.

Pain is a great teacher in many ways; however, pain must only be allowed to visit. If pain is allowed to take up permanent residency in your world, the results can be catastrophic. Pain is unavoidable, inescapable and inevitable, but it should only be allowed to visit because suffering is optional. Every day is not going to be perfect, but every day does have a purpose.

The moments of pain may come from loss and anguish, bereavement and grief, or anxiety and despair. Some people allow pain to be an endless imprisonment, while others find freedom from suffering.

Have you ever wondered how one woman could go through childbirth claiming it was the most painful experience ever, while another woman goes through childbirth and claims it was the most joyful experience of her life? This same concept is true for one person who does not like to exercise, while another person can't wait to get to the gym. It's all about how you relate to being uncomfortable. We must understand that sometimes in life we have to live in pain. Being uncomfortable has a lot to do with growth. But even if the body is ill or has an injury, the soul and spirit still have the ability to experience peace and calm.

So what do we do with pain when it comes upon us? We turn towards it and understand it, rather than turn away and deny it. You must understand it in order to learn from it. Don't carry pain around, but rather, put it under your feet and use it as a stepping stone for growth.

We must also understand pain as a great teacher of life. Pain pushes individuals to ask questions and seek answers. A painful experience has so much to teach us. This does not mean that we should desire pain like a masochist, but rather, when it comes, we should say "hello pain." By avoiding pain, we are neglecting the process of learning how to deal with pain.

If you want to be a champion in the game of life, you must view life as an apprenticeship that you take on along with your formal education. Your teacher may teach and then test you, but the universe will test and then teach you.

Learning is all about participation. Don't get in-line, get on-line, because when you're in-line, you're waiting, but when you're on-line, you're participating.

I value learning above everything else, including money and love. Because it is by my wisdom that I earn money and it is by my wisdom that I value love.

I make sure that dignity be diggin' me. The more your wisdom grows, the bigger capacity you have for pain. Those that don't have the courage to deal with pain fail to gain wisdom.

Some of the greatest minds that ever walked this earth learned how to understand pain, and how to remain gentle, kind and humble even in the midst of pain. If you want to live a rich life, you must learn how to respond to pain, not just react. One must be spiritually fit, psychologically fit and physically fit to deal with pain properly.

In other words, put on your armor. You've got to be dressed-up to get blessed-up. There is a time where pain reaches its supreme point of peace, and it is at that point that you will find understanding and you will realize there is no more pain.

"Now no chastening seems to be joyful for the present, but painful; nevertheless, afterward it yields the peaceable fruit of righteousness to those who have been trained by it." (Hebrew 12:11)[5]

"He is despised and rejected by men, A Man of sorrows and acquainted with grief." (Isaiah 53:3)[6]

Great power, toughness, and strength come over to those who overcome hardship. Remember, you are different than anyone else for a reason. In your pain, you can find the understanding of your reason for being. Failures and mistakes are precisely your means for learning and educating yourself.

Out of your mess comes your message. If you can identify your pain, you can identify your reason. The Spirit of the Universe is not punishing you; He is preparing you. Trust in His plan and not in your pain. The important thing to remember about pain is that you need to be healed from it, because after all, what will not heal, will surely kill.

It's perfectly alright to be angry with the Spirit of the Universe; He can take it. However, do not sin because of your anger and do not go to sleep dirty. Tomorrow is a new day, so do your best to wake up clean.

"'Be angry, and do not sin:' do not let the sun go down on your wrath, nor give place to the devil." (Ephesians 4:26-27)[7]

When all is said and done, I believe that 3 of the most profound reasons we encounter pain are so that we can come to know the Spirit of the Universe, become stronger as an individual on this earth, and learn how to have compassion for others.

"Is there not a time of hard service for man on earth?" (Job 7:1)[8]

If you endure chastening, God deals with you as with sons; for what son is there whom a father does not chasten? But if you are without chastening, of which all have become partakers, then you are illegitimate and not sons. Furthermore, we have had human fathers who corrected us, and we paid them respect. Shall we not much more readily be in subjection to the Father of spirits and live? (Hebrews 12:7-9)[9]

Finally, let me make this point. A storm reveals the foundation of the temple, it does not change the foundation of the temple. It is by the storms of life that you will see what you are made of.

"It is doubtful whether God can bless a man greatly until He has hurt him deeply." – A.W. Tozer[10]

"In a storm do you see God or a Ghost? In your answer lies your faith." – R. R. Bennett, Sr.

Food

: material consisting essentially of protein, carbohydrate, and fat used in the body of an organism to sustain growth, repair, and vital processes and to furnish energy;

: such food together with supplementary substances (as minerals, vitamins, and condiments)

: inorganic substances absorbed by plants in gaseous form or in water solution

: nutriment in solid form

: something that nourishes, sustains, or supplies[1]

"So you shall serve the LORD your God, and He will bless your bread and your water." (Exodus 23:25)[2]

When we think of food we think of the daily activity of eating. There is over-eating, which leads to many health problems that are associated with being overweight, and there is under-eating, which leads to problems such as undernourishment, anorexia, and bulimia. The rich way is to eat a balanced diet.

Food, shelter, and clothing are among the most basic needs of human beings. When basic needs are unmet, people become very motivated to meet those needs, and if those needs continue not to be met, the desire to fulfill those basic needs will become stronger and stronger. For example, the longer a person goes without food, the hungrier they will become, and the more motivated they are to find food.

Food is what people eat. Food is a substance or material that originates in the environment in the form of plants, animals or water, and the human body needs food to survive. The average person can only live 3 weeks without food.

Most people take their bodies for granted, but if you stop and think about it, the human body performs amazing feats every second of the day. The number one reason you need food is that humans get nutrients and energy from the food they eat. Without proper nutrition, your body can't survive.

Food is what helps you grow and develop. The food that you eat should contain the nutrients you need to remain healthy. For example, your body needs certain minerals, which are essential nutrients your body needs but cannot produce.

There are two types of minerals your body needs, macro minerals and trace minerals. Macro minerals are what your body needs in large amounts, and there are seven generally recognized macro minerals: calcium, phosphorus, sulfur, magnesium, potassium, sodium, and chloride. Calcium is the most abundant mineral in the human body and is needed to build strong bones and teeth. Phosphorus is the second most abundant mineral in the human body. It also plays an important role in building strong bones and teeth, as well as repairing cells and producing proteins the body needs. Sulfur is the third most abundant mineral in the human body and a vital component of healthy cartilage. Sulfur is also the sixth most abundant macro mineral in breast milk. The vitamins and minerals listed on the baby's formula can are no match for those in the milk made by mom; don't let the math fool you. There is a bigger picture to look at. Milk, like food, is better when it is closest to its natural form. Magnesium is the fourth most abundant mineral in the human body. Magnesium supports muscle and nerve function, keeps your heart beating regularly, and boosts immunity. Potassium is needed to control the electrical activity of your heart, making it vital to balancing your heart rhythm. Sodium is needed to stimulate nerves, promote healthy muscle function, and maintain the correct balance of fluid in the cells, although it's important to note that too much sodium can increase your risk of developing high blood pressure. Chloride, usually consumed as a salt compound, such as sodium chloride (table salt), balances the fluids in your body and plays a key role in the production of digestive juices in the stomach. However, with the high content of salt in everyday foods, most people meet the daily recommended intake with very little effort, and so sodium intake should be monitored to keep levels in balance.[3]

Trace minerals like zinc, manganese, copper, iron, fluoride, iodine, chromium and selenium, also support important bodily functions but are only needed in small amounts. The best way to get the mineral your body need is by eating a wide variety of foods.[4]

Protein is very important when it comes to building and repairing bones, muscles, and skin. Your body needs protein. Protein can come from many sources including beans, meat and poultry, dairy, and nuts. Of the twenty amino acids found in the protein in your body, nine of those are essential amino acids that cannot be made by the human body, and as a result, they must come from food. The nine essential amino acids are isoleucine, leucine, lysine, methionine, phenylalanine, threonine, tryptophan, valine, histidine.[5]

If you eat enough protein each day (approximately 0.36 grams per pound of body weight for a sedentary person) and choose a variety of protein sources, such as lean meat, low-fat dairy products, beans, nuts, and seeds, your body will obtain each of the nine essential amino acids it needs. Keep in mind that the recommended amount of protein will vary based on each individual's weight, body composition, and activity level.

Protein is not just about quantity; it's also about quality. Generally speaking, eating animal protein provides us with all of the essential amino acids. If you don't eat animal foods, then it's a little more challenging to get all the protein and essential amino acids your body needs, so pay special attention to making sure your protein needs are being met.[6]

Carbohydrates are the body's main source of energy. Your digestive system changes carbohydrates into glucose (a simple sugar), which is converted to energy and used to support bodily functions and physical activity. Your body uses this sugar as energy for your cells, tissues, and organs. Much like protein, the amount of carbohydrates in a diet - high or low - is less important than the quality of carbohydrates in the diet. Carbohydrates are found in both healthy and unhealthy foods. The healthiest sources of carbohydrates are found in unprocessed or minimally processed beans, fruits, vegetables and whole grains. Unhealthy sources of carbohydrates include highly processed or refined foods like white bread, pastries, and sodas to name a few.[7]

Fats help your body absorb vitamins and aid in its growth and development. Most foods contain several different kinds of fat, and some are better for your health than others. Your body makes its own fat from taking in too many calories. Healthy fats that are found in fish, nuts, olive oil and seeds help you to control your cholesterol levels. Fats can also be bad for you. Fats are high in calories, and small amounts can add up fast. If you eat more calories than you need, you will gain weight, and excess body weight is linked to poor health. Saturated fats and trans fats are unhealthy, especially when you eat them often.[8]

Vitamins are substances that your body needs to develop and function normally. Your body needs thirteen types of vitamins, including A, C, D, E, K, and eight types of B vitamins. Without certain vitamins, you may develop medical problems. For example, if you don't get enough vitamin C, you could experience dental problems, such as tooth loss and gum problems. Without enough vitamin D, children may develop rickets, which weakens your bones. The best way to get enough vitamins is to eat a balanced diet. Sometimes people do need to take supplements, though it is always a good idea to check with your health care practitioner first.[9]

Food is nature. In this sense, food is good when it comes from nature and not so good when it doesn't. The more natural food is, the better it is. The more we live in accordance with the Spirit of the Universe's order, the more balanced and rich our life will be. Being in harmony with nature is good and peaceful, and being in disharmony with nature leads to turbulence.

> And the fear of you and the dread of you shall be on every beast of the earth, on every bird of the air, on all that move on the earth, and on all the fish of the sea. They are given into your hand. Every moving thing that lives shall be food for you. I have given you all things, even as the green herbs. But you shall not eat flesh with its life, that is, its blood. (Genesis 9:2-4)[10]

There are certain human duties when it comes to food. We should never eat people or flesh with blood, nor should we allow people to starve. In a very real way, we as human beings have an obligation to prevent starvation by any means necessary. When it comes to ourselves and food, we should eat food not only to survive but to enrich ourselves. Food and drink should be balanced and enjoyed. In a natural way, all food is soul food.

"Go, eat your bread with joy, and drink your wine with a merry heart; for God has already accepted your works." (Ecclesiastes 9:7)[11]

There are 3 food virtues: hospitality, temperance and table manners. The virtue of hospitality is about sharing one's food and drink with people, whether they are relatives, friends or strangers. The virtue of temperance is about how to balance one's food and drink consumption. Do not be a glutton or a drunk, and stop yourself from eating and drinking past the point of comfort. The virtue of table manners is about 3 virtues in itself: cleanliness, appropriate language, and conduct. All of these have nothing to do with what is going into you, but have everything to do with who you are and what comes out of you.

> When He had called all the multitude to Himself, He said to them, "Hear Me, everyone, and understand: There is nothing

that enters a man from outside which can defile him; but the things which come out of him, those are the things that defile a man. If anyone has ears to hear, let him hear!" When He had entered a house away from the crowd, His disciples asked Him concerning the parable. So He said to them, "Are you thus without understanding also? Do you not perceive that whatever enters a man from outside cannot defile him, because it does not enter his heart but his stomach, and is eliminated, thus purifying all foods?" And He said, "What comes out of a man, that defiles a man. For from within, out of the heart of men, proceed evil thoughts, adulteries, fornications, murders, thefts, covetousness, wickedness, deceit, lewdness, an evil eye, blasphemy, pride, foolishness. All these evil things come from within and defile a man." (Mark 7:14-23)[12]

If you are looking for a heart-healthy eating plan, then the Mediterranean diet could be right for you. New research is shedding light on the Mediterranean diet saying it could improve heart and brain functions. The Mediterranean diet, which focuses on vegetables, grains, and olive oil, is unlike the American diet, which is heavy on salty foods, red meat, and sweets.[13]

There is a lot to be learned from food. Food has been known to be cultural. Food has been known to be racial. Food has been known to be religious. There is food for poor people and food for wealthy people. But no matter what else food is known for, food must be known as a necessary component of being balanced. The five food groups of protein, grains, vegetables, fruits, and dairy are the building blocks of a healthy diet.

"But food does not commend us to God; for neither if we eat are we the better, nor if we do not eat are we the worse." (1 Corinthians 8:8)[14]

"Therefore, whether you eat or drink, or whatever you do, do all to the glory of God. Give no offense, either to the Jews or to the Greeks or to the church of God." (1 Corinthians 10:31-32)[15]

"One cannot sleep well, think well or do well if one does not eat well." – R. R. Bennett, Sr.

Shelter

: something that covers or affords protection
: an establishment providing food and shelter
: a position or the state of being covered and protected[1]

Your shelter is your home, and the heart of your home is your family. These 3 go together and are one: shelter, home, and family. A home (household) is where you live permanently, especially as members of a family. In fact, once you no longer live in your parents' home, they become your relatives and are no longer a part of your family in the same sense that those living in the same household are family.

"But if anyone does not provide for his own, and especially for those of his household, he has denied the faith and is worse than an unbeliever." (1 Timothy 5:8)[2]

The one thing that a home should do is shelter you from the harms of the outside world by allowing you to feel safe and deserving even on the worst day, not just physically, but emotionally as well. A home is where you are treated with dignity and respect. I see a home as a place where I feel comfortable cooking breakfast in my pajamas. To be at home is to feel comfortable.

Some people think that a house and a home are the same thing, but that's just not true. A home is personal and a house is literal. A house is a noun for a place of living, grammatically identical to an apartment or other places of living. The word house can also be used as a verb. You can be housed or re-housed. The difference between a house and a home is the fact that you can feel at home or not feel at home in a house. The house is only the structure that you utilize. You don't feel any connection with the physical place, whereas a home has an affective aspect; it is a place where you feel and know you truly belong. You can build a house with materials, but you need love to build a home. A newly built house is clearly not a home. In fact, it is not until after you move into a house that you start building your home.

"Through wisdom a house is built, and by understanding it is established; by knowledge the rooms are filled with all precious and pleasant riches." (Proverbs 24:3-4)[3]

"My people will dwell in a peaceful habitation, in secure dwellings, and in quiet resting places." (Isaiah 32:18)[4]

Some people start building a home without giving it much thought because their lives are so lined up with the Spirit of the Universe that it takes very little effort. But for others, it takes a great deal of effort to build a home. A home is more than a place; it is Spirit, people, feelings, and memories, building on each other like bricks to create a shelter of love to keep the family safe.

Now therefore, fear the LORD, serve Him in sincerity and in truth, and put away the gods which your fathers served on the other side of the River and in Egypt. Serve the LORD! And if it seems evil to you to serve the LORD, choose for yourselves this day whom you will serve, whether the gods which your fathers served that were on the other side of the River, or the gods of the Amorites, in whose land you dwell. But as for me and my house, we will serve the LORD. (Joshua 24:14-15)[5]

Marriage is the foundation of family life and exists in all cultures with some variations. The natural definition of a family is a married father and mother and their children (by blood or adoption) living together under one roof. Now, this definition may not be what you define a family to be, however, it aligns with the natural order of the Spirit of the Universe that is required to balance mankind.

The family is a major social institution. The Spirit of the Universe puts life and love together in order to create a family. In other words, family is where life begins and love never ends. Family is a shelter and a safe haven in its own right for spiritual, mental, emotional and physical support. In fact, there is no better-built shelter than the pavilion of protection, which was built by the Spirit of the Universe for those who were called.

> One thing I have desired of the LORD,
> That will I seek:
> That I may dwell in the house of the LORD
> All the days of my life,
> To behold the beauty of the LORD,
> And to inquire in His temple.
> For in the time of trouble
> He shall hide me in His pavilion;
> In the secret place of His tabernacle
> He shall hide me;
> He shall set me high upon a rock. (Psalm 27:4-5)[6]

> And we know that all things work together for good to those who love God, to those who are the called according to His purpose. For whom He foreknew, He also predestined to be conformed to the image of His Son, that He might be the firstborn among many brethren. Moreover whom He predestined, these He also called; whom He called, these He also justified; and whom He justified, these He also glorified. (Romans 8:28-30)[7]

Living in today's world and having an intimate relationship with the Spirit of the Universe is like being sheltered in the center of a hurricane where there is calm, yet outside, there is a great degree of chaos.

Your family shelter is where you get introduced to morals as well as appropriate behavior and interactions. So much of our personalities, dreams, hopes, and fears come from our family. The family is the primary way we raise children. The family is the most basic, natural and fundamental unit that we most intimately identify with.

Families are very important. No man is an island. We are also social creatures. We need the personal relationships we have with our family members so we can be healthy spiritually, mentally, emotionally and physically. You don't belong everywhere; you belong somewhere. Where you are matters as much as who you are.

Every human being has an assignment. You don't decide your assignment, you discover it. The path that leads to discovery starts with your family. Your assignment is always to a person or a group of people, and the people you are assigned to are the people whose pain you feel and whose enemies you are willing to confront.

Your shelter is your home that is created by marriage, blood or adoption. Your shelter is the place where you are supposed to be. Divine prosperity is also a place. If you want to be rich as I define rich in this book, you must be in the right place. You must be in the right place spiritually, mentally, emotionally and physically because at that right place is the beginning of becoming rich.

Clothing

: garments in general; also coverings[1]

Clothing is what people wear to cover their bodies. Clothing is worn for many reasons. Clothing allows individuals to have a shield of privacy and protection. Clothing is also a way we can communicate with others and identify ourselves. Clothing is a basic need and based on the garments we wear, we can communicate to others our nationality, religion or personality.

"A woman shall not wear anything that pertains to a man, nor shall a man put on a woman's garment, for all who do so are an abomination to the LORD your God." (Deuteronomy 22:5)[2]

Clothing is a basic need in our world for 3 main reasons; physical, psychological and social. The reasons we physically use clothes are for privacy and protection. The reasons we psychologically use clothes are for dignity and respect. The reasons we socially use clothes are for identification and decoration.

Clothing for privacy refers to what a person determines to be appropriate clothing for their body to cover private parts, and is generally influenced by culture or religion. In the United States, nudity in public places is against the law.

As for protection, people don't have a natural protective covering of feathers or fur like many animals do to help protect them from climate and weather. Therefore, people must use clothes as a covering for safety and sanitation.

When it comes to clothing ourselves for psychological reasons, it's about dignity and respect. To have clean clothes to wear is an honor. It boosts self-esteem and is very much a part of our basic needs. People are also socially identified by the clothes they wear and how they use clothes as decoration. Living in the United States and other first world nations allows many people to take everyday clothing for granted. However, for some people of this world neither food, shelter, nor clothing are guaranteed.

Maslow's hierarchy of needs includes five human needs, which are often depicted as hierarchical levels within a pyramid that illustrate the order in which those needs may be met. The five human needs are physiological needs (food, water, warmth, rest), safety needs (security, safety), belongingness and love needs (intimate relationships, friends), esteem needs (prestige and feeling of accomplishment), and self-actualization (achieving one's full potential, including creative activities).[3] It is safe to say that Maslow's hierarchy of needs includes clothing at a very basic level.

However, even after your needs are met, you must understand that it takes discipline to achieve the balance that is needed to be rich. Too much of one thing and not enough of another can cause a disruption that will surely knock you off balance, and whatever richness you had can quickly turn into a state of poverty, be it spiritual, mental, emotional or physical poverty.

The process of becoming rich refers to the discovery and the discipline of balance which should be present throughout a person's life. The "Philosophy of Balance" is all about life management and occurs when a person completely understands their life for what it is. A rich life is about taking nothing for granted and allowing nothing to be wasted. Being rich is not a perfect permanent state, but rather a continuous process of balancing the twenty-seven manifestations of balance. As a person goes through life, they must make the necessary adjustments to remain balanced, which is required if you want to be rich.

Secondary

Selfishness

: concerned excessively or exclusively with oneself: seeking
 or concentrating on one's own advantage, pleasure, or
 well-being without regard for others
: arising from concern with one's own welfare or advantage in
 disregard of others[1]

I define selfishness as self-preservation. The first law of nature
is self-preservation. We were born to live. Every living thing will
fight to survive. People often misunderstand the word selfishness as
it relates to self-preservation. Selfishness, when in its proper place,
has nothing to do with what I define as self-centeredness, which is
to be engrossed in selfishness.

Self-centeredness is the total disregard for other people, places
or things. On the other hand, selfishness is a virtue when coupled
with courage and discipline. To be courageous is to be strong, and
it is discipline that maintains your courage. At the breaking-point
of every virtue, be it patience, honesty, or any other, is courage
and discipline. Selfishness without discipline gives way to either
self-centeredness or instincts (as is the case with animals).

We humans are slaves to our "selfish gene." We have competing genes, some selfless and empathetic, and some selfish and aggressive, and how we act has a lot to do with what gene is winning. We all have some level of selfishness, yet we are not all self-centered.

It is natural to think of yourself first. Before you can help someone else, you must help yourself. My understanding of the word selfish is not in total agreement with Merriam-Webster's definition. I believe my definition of the word, when coupled with Merriam-Webster's definition, is the more complete and precise meaning.

The natural need to survive (self-preservation) is in every living thing. Our freewill gives us the mindset to know that sometimes we must come first. We must realize that self-preservation and freewill act in unity as selfishness, much in the same way that self-preservation and instincts work together in animals.

It is very important to understand the evolution of human beings from instinct to intellect to intuition. Instinct governs the animal. At the most basic level, human beings utilize instinct to navigate this world. Instinct sends the automatic response signals of fight or flight because the predominant emotion of instinct is fear. The gratification impulses of instinct are to satisfy basic needs and desires such as thirst, hunger, sleep, sex, and protection.

Human beings retain animal instincts until the overriding gifts of both freewill and intellect kick in. The Spirit of the Universe has implanted in our souls the gifts of both freewill and intellect. Freewill and intellect should be a balanced marriage that produces the fruit of intelligence, which is the gift needed for making the right choice.

Your freewill is not independent of intellect and your intellect is not independent of freewill. Intellect is used when human beings apply both complex subjective thoughts and complex objective thoughts. Intellect gives us human beings 3 types of sight: hindsight, insight, and foresight. Intuition is for those advanced souls who are consciously aware of directions and warnings that come from the invisible world.

At the beginning of freewill is instinct and at the end of freewill is intellect. The mind is active and the activities of the mind will be followed as the freewill chooses to follow. While a human being's actions can move them towards the ends they set up for themselves, human intellect has a natural power that is ordered by the Spirit of the Universe towards the truth.

If someone disagrees with the fact that intellect is ordered towards the truth, then they are saying that statement is not true, which means they do care about the truth and only want to believe in the truth, which is precisely the point that I am making. And so, human intellect is, in fact, ordered towards the truth.

As for intuition, it is the proper integration of instinct and intellect. The final state of understanding is spiritual and your power lies within your spirit.

There are instinctual levels of survival and there are intellectual levels of survival. The first right for humans is the right of freewill (liberty). Unlike animals, which act mainly on instincts, we humans have freewill and act mainly on intellect. The Spirit of the Universe has dignified us humans with such instinct, freewill and intellect to be the gods of this earth.

I often say that all of man's decisions are based on freewill and responsibility. Selfishness is not about good or evil, but rather, selfishness is about self-preservation. The same selfishness that propels an individual to robbery also propels an individual to righteousness. It is an individual's moral responsibility that divides robbery and righteousness.

Man is guided by his own selfish, independent judgment, regardless of the consequences of his actions. The common man is often referred to as a man with no attributes, however, to be ordinary is an attribute. Ordinary is natural and natural is righteous. The righteous standard of a man is to embrace your responsibilities over recognition from others. Man has been taught that selfishness is the synonym of evil, that it is unnatural rather than natural, that a selfish man does not think or feel for others. But man must find joy within himself first, and this cannot be done without being selfish. Putting someone else's needs before your own for too long will lead to your own demise. If the opposite of selfish is selfless, which means giving everything to others and sacrificing your own needs, how will a truly selfless person survive, let alone thrive?

"But let each one examine his own work, and then he will have rejoicing in himself alone, and not in another. For each one shall bear his own load." (Galatians 6:4-5)[2]

Selfishness is self-preservation, and when you add freewill, it is the reasoning of the mind that provides an individual with the ability to survive. You need to have the "will to live" in order to keep on living. To see selfishness as evil is a perversion, to say the least. Selfishness is an independent matter. Survival is about in-dependence, not dependence. No man is an island. However, an independent man stands alone and is not concerned with others in any primary manner. You need to be independent to survive in this world.

After all is said and done, you only have yourself to rely on, and when it comes to self, you must have a system in place. S-Y-S-T-E-M stands for save yourself some stress, time, energy and money. Your amount of independence is tied directly to your habits, which are a part of your system. Your self-worth and creativity are tied directly to self-actualization.

Self-actualization represents a concept derived from the Humanistic Psychological theory created by an American psychologist, Abraham Maslow. Self-actualization, according to Maslow, represents the growth of an individual towards the fulfillment of the highest needs.[3] Everything that you need in life must draw from the ability to understand self. All that you desire to have starts from within.

Another American psychologist, Carl Rogers, agreed with Maslow's concept of self-actualization, but Rogers believed that a person would not achieve self-actualization unless their real self was congruent with their ideal self. He defined congruence as how closely one's real self matches up with their ideal self, and the more closely they match the higher one's self-worth.

Incongruent

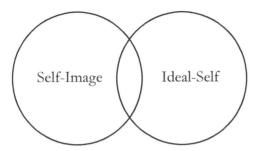

The self-image is different from the ideal self.
There is only a little overlap.
Here self-actualization will be difficult.

Congruent

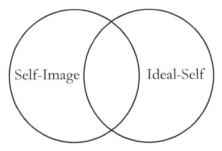

The self-image is similar to the ideal self.
There is more overlap.
This person can self-actualize.   *Self-Actualization Diagram*[4]

The self-concept is comprised of 3 components: self-worth (what we think about ourselves), self-image (how we see ourselves) and the ideal self (the person we would like to be). These concepts are unique to each of us and often change as we move throughout our lives.[4] The real self is comprised of self-worth and self-image.

People who do not understand selfishness as it relates to self-preservation will be pulled away from loving and standing up for themselves, and will most likely spend their life as either a dependent or an enabler, always falling short of their own potential.

A selfish person will not tolerate being bullied by another person, at least not for very long, and in many cases, not at all. A selfish person has no other choice but to be independent; it is a part of their very nature.

Selfishness means you care enough about yourself to meet your own needs. If you are a needy person, then you are not selfish enough. Selfishness is a good thing. It is a virtue.

"Self-fullness" is a term I use to describe how to fill yourself up from the inside and shine brightly on the outside. It is how you balance your real-self and your ideal-self in such a way that they fit together and make sense.

Self-fullness is what you need to be the best version of yourself. You can only get to self-fullness by being selfish. The healthiest, most vibrant people of the world possess a good dose of selfishness. Don't be fooled by those who say or think that selfishness is a disdained human character trait because nothing can be further from the truth. Some people think that selfish people try to keep everything to themselves. However, truly selfish people give more because they have more to give, and by giving, I don't mean only in a monetary way.

"Let each of you look out not only for his own interests, but also for the interests of others." (Philippians 2:4)[5]

Your survival is dependent on your selfishness, which is needed to balance your life and to be rich. To be rich is to be righteous, independent, consistent and healthy. Selfishness means you do not exist for any other person, and you do not ask any other person to exist for you. In other words, selfish people love themselves, because after all, they are selfish.

Repentance

: to turn from sin and dedicate oneself to the amendment of
　　one's life
: to feel regret or contrition
: to change one's mind[1]

Repentance, which literally means to change one's mind, is
the activity of reviewing one's actions and feeling regret for past
wrongs. True repentance is the renewing of the mind that ultimately results in a change of actions.

> For the past 33 years, I have looked in the mirror every morning
> and asked myself: "If today were the last day of my life, would
> I want to do what I am about to do today?" And whenever the
> answer has been "No" for too many days in a row, I know I
> need to change something. – Steve Jobs[2]

The evil-genius is a spirit that each person has within themselves
which tries to negatively influence him or her, and it is in direct
opposition with one's virtuous-genius, which is also in each of us.
This, my beloved, is the battlefield of the mind.

However, an infant is born without sin. A child inherits neither righteousness nor sin; an infant is as pure as heaven.

> Yet you say, "Why should the son not bear the guilt of the
> father?" Because the son has done what is lawful and right,
> and has kept all My statutes and observed them, he shall sure-
> ly live. The soul who sins shall die. The son shall not bear the
> guilt of the father, nor the father bear the guilt of the son. The
> righteousness of the righteous shall be upon himself, and the
> wickedness of the wicked shall be upon himself. (Ezekiel 18:19-
> 20)[3]

But Jesus said, "Let the little children come to Me, and do not
forbid them; for of such is the kingdom of heaven." (Matthew
19:14)[4]

By the time a person has become an adult, he or she has committed many sins. Jesus Christ was the only adult whom Satin was
unable to touch.

"For all have sinned and fall short of the glory of God." (Romans 3:23)[5]

"For we do not have a High Priest who cannot sympathize with
our weaknesses, but was in all points tempted as we are, yet without
sin." (Hebrews 4:15)[6]

"Who committed no sin, nor was deceit found in His mouth."
(1 Peter 2:22)[7]

"And you know that He was manifested to take away our sins,
and in Him there is no sin." (1 John 3:5)[8]

To repent is to admit to one's mistakes. All human beings who
have walked this earth from the past until the present have committed countless sins. Repentance must come from within. To repent
for an hour is better than having not repented at all. Repentance
combined with prayer is so important that it is the necessary requirement to break past the earthly jurisdiction that is set upon the
infidels.

It is important to know that guilt and repentance are not the
same thing. Guilt occurs when you do not forgive yourself. Guilt

is a negative and paralyzing emotion that leads to depression and frustration rather than improvement. Guilt is usually a negative focus on oneself. Guilt is also a psychological weapon often used by one person against another. Guilt is a learned, socially imposed emotion. Guilt is not a basic human emotion, which means you can overcome it by un-learning it. Now, I'm not saying you shouldn't feel regret or remorse about your wrong doings. However, I stress repentance, not guilt. Guilt will make you hate yourself. No one is born to hate, people learn to hate, and if you can learn to hate, you can be taught to love.

Sometimes repentance is all we have. You cannot turn back the hands of time. If you misuse time itself, no matter how much you regret it, you can't get it back. All that is left to make right the wrongs of the past is repentance, so repent and move forward. There is no rest for people who don't understand that they are forgiven and made right by repentance. Because of freewill, we all make mistakes, even when we are trying to do the right thing. If you can see up, get up! Repentance is renewal. There is rest in repentance.

"Come to Me, all you who labor and are heavy laden, and I will give you rest. Take My yoke upon you and learn from Me, for I am gentle and lowly in heart, and you will find rest for your souls. For My yoke is easy and My burden is light." (Matthew 11:28-30)[9]

Where guilt is negative, repentance is positive. Repentance is a very important factor to consider when improving our way of thinking and behaving because repentance is all about correcting our mind, speech, and body. Repentance will improve what we think, what we say, and how we act.

Changing one's mind may be simple, but it sure isn't easy. At first, it may seem like an easy task because most individuals don't realize how much trash has been stored in their minds over the years. Renewing the mind is about getting rid of the trash that exists in your mind. For some people, it is very hard to get rid of the trash that exists in their mind because they don't recognize the trash as trash.

The first step to renewing the mind is to get rid of the trash that you do recognize as trash. Think of your mind as the upper room in your house. Everything that was fed to your mind, trash as well as treasure, exists in your upper room at one time or another, from the first supper to the last supper.

At first, all your trash will not be recognizable as trash. But if you get rid of the trash that you recognize, your thoughts will become clearer. The clearer your thoughts are, the cleaner your upper room will be. The cleaner your upper room, the more you can identify the trash.

Identifying and getting rid of the trash in your upper room is the process of renewing the mind. Beloved, I'm not trying to make sainthood. I'm one of the most flawed people I know. But I am pushing to do the best I can. Renewing the mind is a great process for a flawed man. Repentance helps us to right the wrong. We as human beings must always beware of the evil-genius and the importance of keeping it in check.

Two of the best ways to develop a righteous life are to think right and to refrain from telling lies. Most sins, if not all sins, start or finish with wrong thinking and a lie. The repentant sinner should strive to do right with the same faculties with which he did wrong. With whatever part of the body you did bad deeds, you should now engage in good deeds. A troublemaker should become a peacemaker, a thief should open his hand to charity, and if the mouth spoke lies, let it now speak the truth.

The Spirit of the Universe fully understands the temptations that come our way and that some of us might succumb to those temptations. Only through repentance can we wipe out those sins and past wrong doings and gradually get freed from the clutches of weakness.

Repentance is the most beloved and noble form of obedience in the eyes of the Spirit of the Universe. Repentance has a higher status than any other form of worship. The Spirit of the Universe loves those who repent.

"He who keeps instruction is in the way of life, but he who

refuses correction goes astray." (Proverbs 10:17)[10]

"If My people who are called by My name will humble themselves, and pray and seek My face, and turn from their wicked ways, then I will hear from heaven, and will forgive their sin and heal their land." (2 Chronicles 7:14)[11]

"The time is fulfilled, and the kingdom of God is at hand. Repent, and believe in the gospel." (Mark 1:15)[12]

"Take heed to yourselves. If your brother sins against you, rebuke him; and if he repents, forgive him. And if he sins against you seven times in a day, and seven times in a day returns to you, saying, 'I repent,' you shall forgive him." (Luke 17:3-4)[13]

"If we confess our sins, He is faithful and just to forgive us our sins and to cleanse us from all unrighteousness." (1 John 1:9)[14]

With repentance comes the understanding of forgiveness and its proper place. If you want the Spirit of the Universe to forgive you when you sin, then you must also exercise forgiveness after someone has sinned against you, regardless of whether they repent or not.

Reconciliation requires at least two people, but forgiveness only requires one person. I know, sometimes it is very hard to find forgiveness when someone has wronged you badly or been the cause of a traumatic experience you've suffered. However, my beloved, if you can just be thankful for the experience, you can find forgiveness.

Forgiveness and repentance together have great power to change a life. When a person practices forgiveness and repentance with a pure mind, he cannot fail to change for the good. The revengeful become forgiving. The cruel become compassionate. The greedy become more generous. The restless become more serene. A child of the Spirit of the Universe is a vessel of light, and it is that light that eliminates darkness.

Therefore, as the elect of God, holy and beloved, put on tender mercies, kindness, humility, meekness, longsuffering; bearing with one another, and forgiving one another, if anyone has a complaint against another; even as Christ forgave you, so you also must do. (Colossians 3:12-13)[15]

It is the Spirit of the Universe that leads a person to repentance because repentance and salvation are tied together. Salvation is a gift of justification, which cannot be lost, and that comes by way of repentance. It is something that the Spirit of the Universe gives, and it is only possible because of His grace. The gift of justification cannot be the result of good works because a gift is free. A gift is unlike a crown or prize, which are rewards for works, such as enduring and suffering.

Do you not know that those who run in a race all run, but one receives the prize? Run in such a way that you may obtain it. And everyone who competes for the prize is temperate in all things. Now they do it to obtain a perishable crown, but we for an imperishable crown. Therefore I run thus: not with uncertainty. Thus I fight: not as one who beats the air. But I discipline my body and bring it into subjection, lest, when I have preached to others, I myself should become disqualified. (1 Corinthians 9:24-27)[16]

I have fought the good fight, I have finished the race, I have kept the faith. Finally, there is laid up for me the crown of righteousness, which the LORD, the righteous Judge, will give to me on that Day, and not to me only but also to all who have loved His appearing. (2 Timothy 4:7-8)[17]

The book of Acts especially concentrates on repentance with regard to salvation.

Then Peter said to them, "Repent, and let every one of you be baptized in the name of Jesus Christ for the remission of sins; and you shall receive the gift of the Holy Spirit. For the promise is to you and to your children, and to all who are afar off, as many as the Lord our God will call." (Acts 2:38-39)[18]

"Repent therefore and be converted, that your sins may be blotted out, so that times of refreshing may come from the presence of the Lord." (Acts 3:19)[19]

"When they heard these things they became silent; and they glorified God, saying, 'Then God has also granted to the Gentiles repentance to life.'" (Acts 11:18)[20]

"Truly, these times of ignorance God overlooked, but now commands all men everywhere to repent." (Acts 17:30)[21]

"How I kept back nothing that was helpful, but proclaimed it to you, and taught you publicly and from house to house, testifying to Jews, and also to Greeks, repentance toward God and faith toward our Lord Jesus Christ." (Acts 20:20-21)[22]

"But declared first to those in Damascus and in Jerusalem, and throughout all the region of Judea, and then to the Gentiles, that they should repent, turn to God, and do works befitting repentance." (Acts 26:20)[23]

Repentance should be practiced in the moment without procrastination. When you wrong someone, be swift to apologize to them personally, or the practice of your repentance before the Spirit of the Universe lacks sincerity. When you sin, repent, but if your pride or situation does not allow you to repent in the moment, make sure you find the time to repent later.

Not only should you practice repentance in the moment, but repentance should also be practiced at the end of each day. At the end of each day we should reflect on our day's work and make a note to repent for any wrong doings. By doing this, we go to sleep clean and wake-up clean. By waking up clean, our minds have the clarity that is needed to make righteous decisions throughout the day.

Sin is like walking down a dead-end street with no turn-offs; you must walk all the way back to get off the street of sin. The more you sin, the longer your walk back.

When you are confronted with the identical situation where you previously committed sin, and it lies within your power to commit that sin again, but you do not commit that sin, that is what constitutes complete repentance. Complete repentance is about talking to the Spirit of the Universe as well as listening to the Spirit of the Universe.

Repentance and empathy have everything to do with building moral courage. Without moral courage, our best virtues are lost from lack of use. Both moral courage and physical courage protect, but each in different ways. Physical courage protects the tangible, whereas moral courage protects the less tangible. Physical courage protects property, but moral courage protects principles. Physical courage protects valuables, but moral courage protects virtues. One of the best ways to develop moral courage is by repentance.

Repentance is a form of mental correction, which means you have to change your way of thinking. The eyes are organs of perception. However, perception involves more than physical sight. Human beings are much like an iceberg; ten percent of the mass of the iceberg is what you see above the water line, and the other ninety percent of the iceberg is below the water line. The same is true with human beings. The part of a person you can see only with your eyes represents ten percent of that person. The other ninety percent is comprised of spirituality, mentality, and physicality and lies below the skin's surface. Below the human skin lies the contents of intentions. Beloved, you would do well to ask the Spirit of the Universe for correction, because the corrections of the Spirit of the Universe deal with the inner man.

"Search me, O God, and know my heart; try me, and know my anxieties; and see if there is any wicked way in me, and lead me in the way everlasting." (Psalm 139:23-24)[24]

We must understand what is wrong and we must have the need to do what is right. The world's greed, poverty, violence, and war all stem from a lack of moral courage and leadership. In today's world, it's very hard to stand totally strong morally, because, for the most part, we live in a culture of immorality. Just think about it. We live in a culture that aborts unborn children and executes its prisoners, which to me are the most severe definitions of premeditated murder. If you are truly pro-life, then you must be against both abortion and capital punishment. Moral leadership is about justice. Vision is required to achieve order, balance, and peace for the entire human race, and we can get there, one person at a time, with repentance.

"Stop dancing with the devil and do good for God." – R. R. Bennett, Sr.

The lack of repentance can lead to the deprivation of righteousness. The sinful man, overwhelmed by his sins, will take his place in a miserable state. Regularly committing sin will darken the spirit, harden the soul, and bring pain to the body, whereas repentance will enlighten the spirit, soften the heart, and bring pleasure to the body.

If for any reason your past wrong doings ever try to hold you down after you have repented, it is then you must realize that the person who did those wrong doings no longer exists. It is very important to crucify your flesh from its worldly passions and desires. It is your love for the Spirit of the Universe and His calling that breaks all strongholds. The Spirit of the Universe gives everything, including salvation, to accomplish His comprehensive plan, which renders all adversaries powerless. So believe and have courage, for in those two is your victory.

> And we know that all things work together for good to those who love God, to those who are the called according to His purpose. For whom He foreknew, He also predestined to be conformed to the image of His Son, that He might be the firstborn among many brethren. Moreover whom He predestined, these He also called; whom He called, these He also justified; and whom He justified, these He also glorified. (Romans 8: 28-30)[25]

"And those who are Christ's have crucified the flesh with its passions and desires." (Galatians 5:24)[26]

The devil is a better minister than any of us, yet he is still the devil. The one thing that separates us from him is our ability to repent.

Perfection is a pipe dream on this side of heaven. However, there is always a reason to work on becoming a better you, which will, in turn, make the world a better place. The "Philosophy of Balance" is more about consistency than intensity. There is no end to your temptations this side of heaven, and if one day you wake up and there are no more temptations, that is only because your life on earth is over!

"Repentance allows a person to practice being a better person." – R. R. Bennett, Sr.

"The heart of the matter is how much the Spirit matters." – R. R. Bennett, Sr.

Empathy

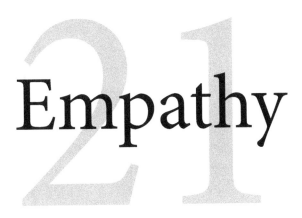

: the imaginative projection of a subjective state into an object
so that the object appears to be infused with it
: the action of understanding, being aware of, being sensitive to,
and vicariously experiencing the feelings, thoughts, and
experience of another of either the past or present without
having the feelings, thoughts, and experience fully commu-
nicated in an objectively explicit manner[1]

Many people confuse empathy with its closely related cousin
sympathy. Although the two qualities are related, there is a difference. When you understand and share the feelings of another for
yourself, you have empathy. When you sympathize with someone,
you have compassion for that person, but you do not necessarily feel their feelings. That is the difference between empathy and
sympathy.

Empathy is the ability to imagine what someone else might be
thinking and feeling. Empathy is deeply rooted in our brains and
bodies. The foundation of compassion is a part of our biological
wiring. At around 18 months, children begin to understand that
other people have feelings different from their own, which is the

necessary precursor to empathy. Elementary forms of empathy have even been observed in our primate relatives, as well as in dogs.

Empathy is a building block to morality. If one would take a good look at what Jesus taught in His "Sermon on the Mount," specifically the part that is called the "Golden Rule," one can begin to understand empathy. The "Golden Rule" is a moral principle of altruism found in nearly every human culture and religion and is related to the basic fundamentals of human nature.

"Therefore, whatever you want men to do to you, do also to them, for this is the Law and the Prophets." (Matthew 7:12)[2]

In order to follow the "Golden Rule," it helps to put yourself in someone else's shoes. You can't begin to do the right thing if you have no idea what the right thing is. Empathy is something we sometimes have limited control over. This is why we often get emotional about fictional characters in a movie we are watching. Although we all have a basic degree of empathy, like talent, it only gets better or stronger when practiced. Empathy is a mindset that can be learned and improved with practice.

The practice of empathy is the key to reducing levels of aggression among children and adults. It is fundamental to resolving conflicts and combating inequality. Teaching empathy to children is a way to focus on their social and emotional development. A great education is much more than English, Math, Science, and Technology. The reason bullying is so problematic in schools today is that many children don't know how to empathize. Furthermore, many of the bullying episodes have on-lookers who are also being adversely affected. This is why it is so important that children are raised with the skills to understand how others might feel and to develop a sense of social responsibility for each other.

Empathy reduces bullying, prejudice, and racism. Teaching empathy to children helps increase their social and emotional knowledge as well as positive social behavior (such as helping and including others) while at the same time decreasing aggression. All of mankind needs to learn how to be righteous global citizens.

Empathy is the main ingredient to any successful relationship because it helps us to understand the other person's perspectives, needs, and intentions. Empathy is good for marriage. Being able to understand your partner's emotions helps to deepen intimacy and allows relationship satisfaction to grow.

Curiosity is the key to learning how to be empathetic. You have to be inquisitive about other people's thinking and feelings, even if you don't agree with them. To better develop your own empathy you have to practice shutting down your inner voice while listening to other people every chance you get. In other words, you have to get out of your own way.

It is not easy to do really well, but well worth doing really well. It is important to realize that you have two ears and one mouth, and therefore should use them accordingly; listen at least twice as much as you speak. An empathetic person will work to support others while not jumping to conclusions about others without any facts.

> Jesus said to him, "You shall love the Lord your God with all your heart, with all your soul, and with all your mind." This is the first and great commandment. And the second is like it: "You shall love your neighbor as yourself." On these two commandments hang all the Law and the Prophets. (Matthew 22:37-40)[3]

> "Rejoice with those who rejoice, and weep with those who weep. Be of the same mind toward one another." (Romans 12:15-16)[4]

Let's kick greed out and let empathy in. It is time to lean forward to the united movement of unity. The global financial crisis of 2008 has allowed people to realize the injustice of the unequal income distribution that has taken place for more than thirty years and has resulted in the drastic shrinking of the middle class.

Billionaires need to make sure they do their part. There is nothing wrong with being wealthy and powerful, but they must not misuse their influence. There are righteous billionaires and wrongful billionaires. Generally speaking, the wrongful billionaires (those who lack empathy) are people who come from industries such as oil and real estate that require certain government connections in order to get their projects approved. These billionaires know how to "game the system" to create wealth, usually at the expense of others, or society in general.

The righteous billionaires typically come from fields of innovation and inventions of technologies. All that I am saying is that with more empathy the world will be a better place.

Today in the United States of America, if you are a Black American Christian, you can be murdered while praying in church, just for being born Black. Remember the Emanuel African Methodist Episcopal Church in Charleston, South Carolina. That incident alone proves that it is always time to work hard for a better human society.

There are many instances in the history of the United States where a severe lack of empathy can be found. The story of the Native Americans is a story marked mainly by betrayal and greed. I find it very sad that the people who were in this land first are the ones who have been most shortchanged in the United States over the years.

We also must look at the middle aged white man, who from the outside, might look to have many advantages. However, in recent years, his life has been uprooted by cultural changes as well as changes in technology.

In the case of immigrants who come and live in this land without the proper papers, they are undocumented immigrants, not illegal immigrants. On this earth, there is no such thing as an illegal human being. Fight ignorance, not immigrants. We all are minorities in one way or another; it just depends on how you slice the pie. Every single person in this world should be invested in the unity of the world. Jesus says we should love our neighbors as ourselves.

Also, we citizens of the United States of America must realize that the criminal justice system treats people better if they are wealthy and guilty then if they are poor and innocent. It's very important that the United States is a nation of laws, not a nation of men. No American citizen is more American than any other American citizen. It does not matter if the wrongs have been done to the white working class, Blacks, the Native Americans or the poor brown people. Empathy is the building block needed to correct these wrongs.

If you are of the mindset that wants America to be great, just remember that before anything can be great, it must be good first, and by good I mean righteous. The wrongful must get knocked down by the righteous, the bad must get pushed back by the good, and the good must make its way to being great. It may not be that easy, but it is that simple.

Empathy is the key to making our society better. Nature is full of examples of empathy and cooperation. Many animals survive not by eliminating each other or keeping everything to themselves, but by sharing. It is far easier to show love and to act with empathy than to be angry and act with aggression.

There are 3 levels of empathy. The first level is empathetic contagion. In the same way that consciousness is contagious, so too, is empathy. Empathetic contagion is when empathy links a group of people during a dramatic event, such as September 11, 2001. The next level is empathetic feelings, which is when you feel for another person as they work through their predicament. The third level is empathetic helping, which is when you act to help another person. What we human beings must understand is that caring and sharing are very much a part of our biological nature. Therefore, we do well when we stay in-tune with ourselves.

Finally, all of you be of one mind, having compassion for one another; love as brothers, be tenderhearted, be courteous; not returning evil for evil or reviling for reviling, but on the contrary blessing, knowing that you were called to this, that you may inherit a blessing.
For "He who would love life and see good days,
Let him refrain his tongue from evil,
And his lips from speaking deceit.

Let him turn away from evil and do good;
Let him seek peace and pursue it.
For the eyes of the Lord are on the righteous,
And His ears are open to their prayers;
But the face of the Lord is against those who do evil." (1 Peter 3:8-12)[5]

There are 3 types of lust that lure us away from the Spirit of the Universe and righteous conduct: lust of the flesh, lust of the eyes, and lust for the pride of life. These were also the 3 ways that Eve was tempted in the garden as well as the 3 different temptations that Jesus experienced.

"So when the woman saw that the tree was good for food, that it was pleasant to the eyes, and a tree desirable to make one wise, she took of its fruit and ate." (Genesis 3:6)[6]

Then Jesus, being filled with the Holy Spirit, returned from the Jordan and was led by the Spirit into the wilderness, being tempted for forty days by the devil. And in those days He ate nothing, and afterward, when they had ended, He was hungry. And the devil said to Him, "If You are the Son of God, command this stone to become bread." But Jesus answered him, saying, "It is written, 'Man shall not live by bread alone, but by every word of God.'" Then the devil, taking Him up on a high mountain, showed Him all the kingdoms of the world in a moment of time. And the devil said to Him, "All this authority I will give You, and their glory; for this has been delivered to me, and I give it to whomever I wish. Therefore, if You will worship before me, all will be Yours." And Jesus answered and said to him, "Get behind Me, Satan! For it is written, 'You shall worship the LORD your God, and Him only you shall serve.'" Then he brought Him to Jerusalem, set Him on the pinnacle of the temple, and said to Him, "If You are the Son of God, throw Yourself down from here. For it is written: 'He shall give His angels charge over you, To keep you,' and, 'In their hands they shall bear you up, Lest you dash your foot against a stone.'" And Jesus answered and said to him, "It has been said, 'You shall not tempt the LORD your God.'" Now when the devil had ended every temptation, he departed from Him until an opportune time. (Luke 4:1-13)[7]

If we want to build and maintain a balanced and caring society, we must develop a relationship with the Spirit of the Universe that will lead to righteous conduct and with the empathy that lies in the souls of ourselves and our children. There must be a vision of justice that celebrates diversity and is inclusive and dedicated to the spiritual, intellectual, emotional, physical, and social growth of all people. The right amount of empathy leads to the growth and peace of civilization, while the lack of empathy could lead to the end of civilization.

"Each man's life touches so many other lives." – Clarence, *It's A Wonderful Life*

"An imbalance between the people is disharmony to the world." – R. R. Bennett, Sr.

Charity

: benevolent goodwill toward or love of humanity
: generosity and helpfulness especially toward the needy or suffering
: aid given to those in need
: a gift for public benevolent purposes[1]

Charity extends by and up to the love of the Spirit of the Universe, but also extends to the love of our neighbors. Charity unites us with the Spirit of the Universe and is of the most basic but excellent of the virtues. The existence of countless hungry, poor and thirsty people in the world points to the need for the teaching of charity to be put into practice. The Spirit of the Universe is always watching, and your charity will stand in the way of calamity. Charity serves as a way to bring balance to every society and to every community.

"Come, you blessed of My Father, inherit the kingdom prepared for you from the foundation of the world: for I was hungry and you gave Me food; I was thirsty and you gave Me drink; I was a stranger and you took Me in; I was naked and you clothed Me; I was sick and you visited Me; I was in prison and you came to Me." Then the righteous will answer Him, saying, "Lord, when did we see You hungry and feed You, or thirsty and give You drink? When did we see You a stranger and take You in, or naked and clothe You? Or when did we see You sick, or in prison, and come to You?" And the King will answer and say to them, "Assuredly, I say to you, inasmuch as you did it to one of the least of these My brethren, you did it to Me." (Matthew 25:34-40)[2]

So now, brethren, I commend you to God and to the word of His grace, which is able to build you up and give you an inheritance among all those who are sanctified. I have coveted no one's silver or gold or apparel. Yes, you yourselves know that these hands have provided for my necessities, and for those who were with me. I have shown you in every way, by laboring like this, that you must support the weak. And remember the words of the Lord Jesus, that He said, "It is more blessed to give than to receive." (Acts 20:32-35)[3]

There is a difference between giving as an act of generosity and giving as an act of charity. With generosity, a person gives out of compassion or kindness when that person realizes that someone is in need of help and that he or she has the ability to help. Charity, on the other hand, is a virtue. With charity, a person gives as a way to cultivate the virtue of charity. By practicing charity, a person has the ability to reduce their own self-centeredness. Our motivation for giving to others is at least as important as the gift itself, so we must be mindful of our motivation for giving. If one believes they might be intimidated or shamed, or that they may potentially receive a favor as the result of a gift or the lack of a gift, and the gift is given as a result of this belief, then they are giving with impure motives. Charity, in its purest form, is a virtue that leads us to a better relationship with the Spirit of the Universe, a relationship that is required to be rich.

"For you know the grace of our Lord Jesus Christ, that though He was rich, yet for your sakes He became poor, that you through His poverty might become rich." (2 Corinthians 8:9)[4]

Charity, at its very core, is the ability to give something and not expect anything in return. If a person expects some material benefit to arise out of their charity, that person is only performing an act of bartering.

It is important to understand that there is no giving without receiving. The two rise together, because ultimately, the giver and the receiver are one. It is only by circumstances that a person is allowed to have the upper hand or lower hand. Charity cannot occur without both the giver and the receiver, so both are equally important, and both are necessary. The true act of charity has no strings attached and leaves both the giver and the receiver free as they take part in one unifying cause. There is no separation of the giver, the gift, or the receiver.

When charity is perfect, there is no loss or gain. There are many ways for a person to practice charity. You can give food to feed the hungry, clothes to clothe the naked or money to help the poor. You can give your blood or give a kidney. You can give knowledge, skill or time to projects that can help better other people's lives.

I do not just recommend charity. I believe charity to be a personal responsibility of every financially stable human being on the planet earth. The practice of charity is universally recognized as one of the most basic human virtues, a quality that testifies to the depth of one's humanity and one's capacity for self-transcendence.

Charity is highly praised by every religion of love and should be practiced regularly. Like prayer, which is an individual responsibility, charity expresses a person's worship of and thanksgiving to the Spirit of the Universe by supporting those in need. Wealth is a gift from the Spirit of the Universe and is provided to people so they can take care of it responsibly and give a portion of it to all living things on earth that are in need, be it man, animal or plant.

"But whoever has this world's goods, and sees his brother in need, and shuts up his heart from him, how does the love of God abide in him?" (1 John 3:17)[5]

Beloved, if you believe in your spirit that the Spirit of the Universe has blessed you with a gift, no matter what that gift may be, you would do well to ask the Spirit of the Universe what way you should be using your gift for the betterment of mankind.

"Be hospitable to one another without grumbling. As each one has received a gift, minister it to one another, as good stewards of the manifold grace of God." (1 Peter 4:9-10)[6]

"If you extend your soul to the hungry and satisfy the afflicted soul, then your light shall dawn in the darkness, and your darkness shall be as the noonday." (Isaiah 58:10)[7]

Charity should be used to support the poor and the needy and to free the prisoners. Charity is a form of righteous anger. We need to be angry when someone is not afforded basic human needs or is mistreated, and we must do what we can to make things better. Take, for example, the current standards of prison sentencing. America needs to stop treating people they are upset with (non-violent offenders) the same way they treat people they fear (violent offenders). Wealthy people, generally speaking, and within reason, are going to be alright when they encounter the justice system. On the other hand, poor people get it bad both coming and going.

> "Be angry, and do not sin:" do not let the sun go down on your wrath, nor give place to the devil. Let him who stole steal no longer, but rather let him labor, working with his hands what is good, that he may have something to give him who has need. Let no corrupt word proceed out of your mouth, but what is good for necessary edification, that it may impart grace to the hearers. And do not grieve the Holy Spirit of God, by whom you were sealed for the day of redemption. Let all bitterness, wrath, anger, clamor, and evil speaking be put away from you, with all malice. And be kind to one another, tenderhearted, forgiving one another, even as God in Christ forgave you. (Ephesians 4:26-32)[8]

Slavery is the original sin of the United States of America. Many people may believe that slavery is dead in the United States of America today. However, the residue of slavery still exists. Slavery breeds racism, racist and corrupt government policies make ghettos, and ghettos supply the prison system, which is nothing more than a modernized institution of slavery. Slavery isn't dead; it has just changed form. In other words, some people are in prison because they are criminals at heart, while others are just victims of circumstance, and both instances are prongs of slavery. For some classes of people, liberty has yet to come.

"While they promise them liberty, they themselves are slaves of corruption; for by whom a person is overcome, by him also he is brought into bondage." (2 Peter 2:19)[9]

With charity, we can free the slaves, feed the hungry, put clothing on the naked and educate the ignorant. The more a person helps someone in need, the more the Spirit of the Universe helps that person. A person who is pursuing spiritual growth must reduce any self-centeredness as well as any strong desire that relates to greed.

Charity is a way to help purify one's soul from the love of money. One must be mindful of any strong attachment to possessions and vices, and make a point to reduce these attachments, as they may lead to enslavement. I view charity as an act of reducing personal greed, which is an unbalanced mental state that hinders spiritual progress. Spiritual progress allows a person to engage in a delicate balancing act, which has the ability to make them rich.

What does it profit, my brethren, if someone says he has faith but does not have works? Can faith save him? If a brother or sister is naked and destitute of daily food, and one of you says to them, "Depart in peace, be warmed and filled," but you do not give them the things which are needed for the body, what does it profit? Thus also faith by itself, if it does not have works, is dead. (James 2:14-17)[10]

Charity is a purifying and refining practice on the path to spiritual progress and balance. Being rich has nothing to do with having too much. Being rich is all about balance. Sometimes we are overloaded with gifts, and it is only by the giving of those gifts that we can find the balance needed to be rich. If you really want fulfillment, you must realize it is not achieved by taking from others but rather by sharing with them. At the end of the day, it is what it is, and you get what you give.

"Service to others is the rent you pay for your room here on earth." – Muhammad Ali[11]

Cooperation

: the action of cooperating, common effort
: association of persons for common benefit[1]

The cooperation of all people, regardless of their ethnic background, is the foundation of achieving peace in the world. As far as I'm concerned, there is only one race in this world and that race is the human race. It is the cooperation of individuals that allows a group of individuals to see the oneness of us all. No one should be discriminated against based on how they look; that is just stupidity at its core. Complexion doesn't mean a thing. Those of us who are spiritually aware know that it is what's on the inside of a person that truly counts. To come together and unify as one of the same breath is the work of the great peace that leads to being rich.

"But the Lord said to Samuel, 'Do not look at his appearance or at his physical stature, because I have refused him. For the Lord does not see as man sees; for man looks at the outward appearance, but the Lord looks at the heart.'" (1 Samuel 16:7)[2]

"Behold, how good and how pleasant it is for brethren to dwell together in unity!" (Psalm 133:1)3

When it comes to racism, it is important to realize that there are

3 different levels of racism. The first level of racism is mental racism, which is made up of all the bias and prejudice you have within yourself. The second level of racism is physical racism, which is when your mental racism is manifested and becomes active towards another person or group of people. The third level of racism is systemic racism, which is racism as a societal structure or institution. In order to tackle racism, you must attack it on all 3 levels. We must mentally attack racism, we must physically attack racism, and we must systematically attack racism.

"Be of the same mind toward one another. Do not set your mind on high things, but associate with the humble." (Romans 12:16)[4]

Systemic racism is the child of slavery. Systemic racism is not rhetoric, it's a reality, and you can't keep reality from being real. Systemic racism is a fact. The United States of America was founded in racism, as the Constitution classified Black people as property. It is this legal recognition of slavery that is the foundation of the racial social systems that have oppressed Blacks in the United States for hundreds of years.

Any sane and just person can see there are systems in place that have unjustly denied Blacks equal treatment as human beings. Systemic racism is about creating structured systems that rationalize and maintain white power and privilege. Over the years, systemic racism has created a complex array of anti-Black structures in the United States that unjustly help whites gain political and economic power. Thanks to the many civil rights activists of all colors and creeds, there has been some progress towards achieving equal rights for all. However, there is still much work that needs to be done.

We all must cooperate to make sure that everyone is treated equally under the law regardless of their gender, national origin, color, ethnicity, religion, sexual preference or disabilities. Equality before the law is one of the basic principles of liberalism. The first right given by the Spirit of the Universe to all of mankind is the right of freewill (liberty).

Righteous people are not born, righteous people are taught to do right. The truth doesn't always come in real time; sometimes it comes in seasons and sometimes you need help understanding the truth.

President Abraham Lincoln started out on the wrong side of the slavery question but Fredrick Douglas helped him get on the right side. President Lyndon Johnson was terrible on race relations yet Dr. Martin Luther King Jr. helped him understand and get it right. The burden of the oppressed is not to make the bystander comfortable. If you have no interest in removing oppression then you have no right to critique those who do. There will always be a need to work towards equal rights for all.

Hatred is degrading and vengeance is demeaning; they are diseases that we must rid our world of. We, the people, must understand that diversity is an asset not a liability. Steve Jobs, who was born a United States citizen, was one of the most successful people in the world and his biological father was a Syrian refugee. People from different ethnic backgrounds working together is a good thing. A contest of ideas is a good thing. Democracy isn't a spectator sport; it's for all the players to get on the field and play the game with equality.

Understanding prejudice is important when applying the practice of cooperation. There is a direct link between prejudice and stereotypes. They often go hand-in-hand, and both can lead to an act of discrimination. In other words, prejudice, stereotypes, and discrimination are distinctly different from one another, however, in today's world they often occur together and in our every day lives. A firm, direct, and explicit way of thinking that does not allow for compromise is the main ingredient in becoming prejudiced.

A separatist believes in separation without wavering at one level or another. The human mind likes to think with the aid of categories and labels. Therefore, it is not easy to think inclusively. Categories are the foundation for prejudgments. However, with the right thinking, we allow categories to overlap to the point of cooperation, rather than allowing categories to be totally separate. Even between life and death, there is no hard and fast line of separation, but rather a fuzzy transformational line.

Separation is the enemy to cooperation. Separation can only happen when there are at least two separate things. In reality, there is no such thing as an individual separate self. Separation comes from the habit of the mind that sorts the world into the categories of "me," "us" and "everybody else." Separation leads to possessiveness and the tendency to manipulate people and things to your own personal advantage. This mindset is an example of anti-social behavior that is characterized by a pattern of a disregard for other people's liberty, often crossing the line of appropriateness and disrespecting other people's rights as human beings.

Separation and anti-social behavior are the same in several ways. First and foremost, they are learned behaviors. They usually begin in childhood and continue into adulthood. People who exhibit these behaviors lack empathy and remorse, and therefore, in many ways, fail to see the hardship endured by others. Women are cultivators by nature and tend to better understand the importance of cooperation. For this reason, these types of separatist views and antisocial behaviors tend to be more prevalent in males than females.

To cooperate is to realize that nothing is truly separate. We can all live better lives and rich lives when we work together as one. Cooperation in the classroom is one of many great ways to teach students to come together and work together to maximize not only their own learning but also that of every student in the classroom. A cooperative classroom allows the classroom to be one community with no separating categories of smart, dumb, black, brown or white, thus allowing each student to learn that they are a part of one another. This is important because it provides a real life scenario where nothing is completely separated, and nothing is simply black, brown or white.

Anyone who takes an honest look at Africa will recognize that its land is the source of our common humanity. The reason why many people have had such negative stereotypes of Africa is because of slavery and colonialism. Slavery and colonialism created a fictional narrative that portrays Africans as unintelligent animal like creatures with no social abilities, no creative skills, and often no way to assimilate into a civilized society. This stereotype was often perpetuated in various novels and films such *Tarzan* (1932)[5] and *The Birth of a Nation* (1915).[6]

Africa is not only the source of humanity but also of scientific innovation and artistic imagination. The Great Pyramid of Khufu at Giza is one of the Seven Wonders of the Ancient World and was built in Africa around 2550 B. C. It is one of the most famous and iconic buildings in the entire world. The Great Pyramid of Giza is the oldest and largest pyramid and would remain the tallest building on earth for about 3,800 years.[7]

Even the whitest of Americans must realize that if they could trace their lineage back to the very beginning, just like Blacks, they too, will end up in a land called Africa. Likewise, many Blacks in the United States today have some white ancestry. There is no pure race, but rather pure human beings. Black people, brown people, and white people are not a division of 3 different types of people, but rather a continuum of one people with a great need to cooperate and unify as one.

"We may have all come on different ships, but we're in the same boat now." – Dr. Martin Luther King Jr.[8]

I believe the word socialist gets an unfairly bad name in the United States of America. I am a registered Democrat, but I have voted for Republicans, which means I put people before party. I am not on the red team or the blue team; I am on the people's team because it is there that I see what is fair and balanced. In fact, I believe given the right information, a socialist and a nationalist will likely agree more than they disagree. However, let me make myself perfectly clear, I am not a nationalist, nor am I a socialist.

Socialism, in a sense, has to be perfect to work. Capitalism doesn't have to be perfect to work, but can be successful with the right amount of socialism. In other words, capitalism and socialism should balance each other. We have a system in place that allows a billionaire to pay fourteen percent or lower in taxes while his secretary pays twenty-eight percent in taxes. I call that greedy and unfair, and most definitely unbalanced. The tax laws in the United States need to be changed to be more fair and balanced. If the politician you voted for ran on cutting social programs for the poor as well as cutting taxes for the wealthy, don't be surprised when the homeless population grows, police officers and teachers get laid-off, and the bridge you drive over every day suddenly collapses.

Voting is an easy process, people. You vote for the person who you feel can get more of the important things done, better than the other person. To indulge in the illusion that with your vote you are going to be delivered by a single savior is a horrendous recipe for political disappointment. Vote for the candidate who represents more of your views and vote against those who represent less of your views. You are not voting against the almighty, you're voting against the alternative. Voting may be easy, but it is serious.

The president of the United States, although just one person, has the diplomatic power, government power, and military power to change the course of history. When you read history, it is plain to see that it only takes one person to have a negative or positive impact on the world. One hyper person with power is something we must always take seriously. So take your vote seriously. It does not matter if that person is a Democrat, Independent, Republican, black, brown or white, you need to vote for the candidate you think will take your views to the White House and will have a positive impact not only on your life but also on the world.

In the past, our government policies leaned toward benefiting white men. Today, we as a country must lean forward and push towards government policies that incorporate women and people of all colors along with white men. I believe that the United States, as one of the wealthiest country in the world, should rebuild its infrastructure and expand its social programs.

Some of the most important social programs in our country are Social Security and Medicare. The free market system does not work when applied to health care. Therefore, I believe that the Medicare our seniors get should be expanded to all Americans as a single-payer health care system, thus making it universal healthcare.

The single-payer health care system puts everybody into the risk pool. So, while one hundred percent of the population has maternity coverage only a potential (and approximate) fifty percent of them can have babies. The same is true with coverage for prostate cancer treatment. One hundred percent of the population has coverage, but less than fifty percent of the population will ever require treatment. This lowers the cost for everyone because there are those in the risk pool who will never utilize every coverage option.

Why do we have to pay for health insurance? I thought the concept of insurance was that you get insurance for things you are unsure of. You get car insurance just in case you get in a car accident. You get home owner's insurance just in case something bad happens to your home. Living, needing health care, getting sick, and someday dying, are guaranteed to happen to us all. It is not something we are unsure of. Health care in the United States of America should not be a privilege, but a human right, like clean drinking water, not something that should be bought and paid for as a commodity.

Most major countries on earth, whether it's the United Kingdom, France or Canada, have managed to provide health care as a right for every citizen, and those countries are spending less money on healthcare per capita than we are.[9] There should be free health care for all Americans. The people in this country who are opposed to this idea need to be more understanding and stop saying it's all about people getting free stuff.

In today's world, providing our students with an education that covers content from kindergarten through twelfth grade is no longer sufficient. Everybody understands and agrees that our education system needs to produce a well-educated workforce. However, what was sufficient thirty, forty, and fifty years ago is no longer sufficient. Therefore, I believe that public education should be expanded to include two years of community college. I believe the United States government has an important role to play in educating its citizens and providing every one of them with the best education possible regardless of their income or the color of their skin. Public community college should be tuition free and a part of the basic education of our youth. If this country is going to be better, then it must do better by supplying free healthcare and public community college education to all of its citizens.

This is not a Democratic thing or a Republican thing, but a better functioning United States thing. These are not radical ideas as much as they are smart ideas that will allow the whole of America to cooperate as one and to be great as one. At first, the revolution starts in the mind, then it develops a body, and then that body grows legs and begins to walk. But make no mistake about it, every step will come at a price because nothing worth having is free. Change comes at a price, balance comes with a process, and unity is all about cooperation.

The righteous people of this world realize that sometimes the mere telling of the truth can be considered a revolutionary act. However, there is no better revolution than the one that has the foundation of truth.

The world's 3 most popular religions of Judaism, Christianity, and Islam are often seen by many as having separate doctrines, and it is this belief in separation that has led to much violence and bloodshed. There have been centuries of bitterness and disagreements between these 3 religions. However, if one would take a profound look at the 3 religions, one would understand how much the doctrine of all 3 religions overlaps with one another. That is why I consider them all to be "People of the Book."

Judaism is the religion of the Jewish people. Their main religious text is the Torah. The Torah refers to the five books of Moses: Genesis, Exodus, Leviticus, Numbers, and Deuteronomy. In the Torah are the stories of Adam and Eve, Noah, Abraham, and Moses, all of whom were prophets and as well as very familiar to both Christians and Muslims. In fact, both Christians and Muslims view the Torah as the word of God/Allah, which was handed down to all of mankind. Judaism believes in the coming of a Messiah, who will be a man who will be king of the earth, and who will bring peace to the nations of this world but will not be Divine. This mortal Messiah has 3 specific things to do: reconstitute the Jewish kingdom, bring about peace with the neighbors and last, but not least, rebuild the Temple.

Christianity is the religion of those who follow the teaching of Jesus Christ, and it builds on the foundation laid down by Judaism. However, the standards that Christians are to follow are much higher than Old Testament law. Old Testament laws judges by the exact letter of the law, and is based on works rather than people's thoughts and attitudes, which are things that others cannot see. Jesus fulfilled and expanded on the Old Testament law by obeying the law not only in works but also in thoughts and intentions.

> Do not think that I came to destroy the Law or the Prophets. I did not come to destroy but to fulfill. For assuredly, I say to you, till heaven and earth pass away, one jot or one tittle will by no means pass from the law till all is fulfilled. Whoever therefore breaks one of the least of these commandments, and teaches men so, shall be called least in the kingdom of heaven; but whoever does and teaches them, he shall be called great in the kingdom of heaven. For I say to you, that unless your righteousness exceeds the righteousness of the scribes and Pharisees, you will by no means enter the kingdom of heaven. (Matthew 5:17-20)[10]

There are over two billion Christians worldwide. Like Jews and Muslims, Christians practice monotheism. Christians believe Jesus to be the Messiah, born of the Virgin Mary and the Son of God, and the Savior of all of mankind. However, Jews, as well as Muslims, do not consider Jesus to be Divine.

Islam is the religion that is practiced by Muslims. Like Christians, Muslims are very much aware of Mary and Jesus and speak of them both with reverence and respect. However, Jewish people reject Jesus as the Messiah. According to the Quran, Jesus was born miraculously by the will of the Allah without a father and is respected as a Prophet. The Quran states clearly that Jesus was the result of a virgin birth.

Abraham is the unifying figure who transcends the differences among Jews, Christians and Muslims. The careful, balanced message of the story of Abraham is that the Spirit of the Universe loves all His children, and that message existed long before any religion existed.

One of the first countries in the world to become Christian was Ethiopia and Judaism was practiced in Ethiopia long before Christianity.

Now an angel of the Lord spoke to Philip, saying, "Arise and go toward the south along the road which goes down from Jerusalem to Gaza." This is desert. So he arose and went. And behold, a man of Ethiopia, a eunuch of great authority under Candace the queen of the Ethiopians, who had charge of all her treasury, and had come to Jerusalem to worship, was returning. And sitting in his chariot, he was reading Isaiah the prophet. Then the Spirit said to Philip, "Go near and overtake this chariot." So Philip ran to him, and heard him reading the prophet Isaiah, and said, "Do you understand what you are reading?" And he said, "How can I, unless someone guides me?" And he asked Philip to come up and sit with him. The place in the Scripture which he read was this:

"He was led as a sheep to the slaughter;
And as a lamb before its shearer is silent,
So He opened not His mouth.
In His humiliation His justice was taken away,
And who will declare His generation?
For His life is taken from the earth."

So the eunuch answered Philip and said, "I ask you, of whom does the prophet say this, of himself or of some other man?" Then Philip opened his mouth, and beginning at this Scripture, preached Jesus to him. Now as they went down the road, they came to some water. And the eunuch said, "See, here is water. What hinders me from being baptized?" Then Philip said, "If you believe with all your heart, you may." And he answered and said, "I believe that Jesus Christ is the Son of God." So he commanded the chariot to stand still. And both Philip and the eunuch went down into the water, and he baptized him. Now when they came up out of the water, the Spirit of the Lord caught Philip away, so that the eunuch saw him no more; and he went on his way rejoicing. (Acts 8:26-39)[11]

At some Ethiopian festivals, two lambs must be slaughtered, and one lamb gets the Halal treatment for Muslims, while the other lamb is for the Christians. Many people don't realize that in much of Ethiopia, Christians and Muslims live side by side. There is a peaceful history of cooperation that the Ethiopians are quite proud of. The Christians came to Ethiopia during the time of the Apostles, which was the very beginning of Christianity. It has been said that Muslims, after being persecuted for believing that "Allah is one," were driven from Mecca. They sought sanctuary in Abyssinia (modern day Ethiopia) which was then ruled by a Christian king, who was well-known for being a just and God-fearing man. As you can see from this example, people who practice different religions truly do have the ability to cooperate with one another. If Billy Crystal, a Jew, and Muhammad Ali, a Muslim, can love each other like brothers, then so too, can the rest of the world.

Receive one who is weak in the faith, but not to disputes over doubtful things. For one believes he may eat all things, but he who is weak eats only vegetables. Let not him who eats despise him who does not eat, and let not him who does not eat judge him who eats; for God has received him. Who are you to judge another's servant? To his own master he stands or falls. Indeed, he will be made to stand, for God is able to make him stand. One person esteems one day above another; another esteems every day alike. Let each be fully convinced in his own mind. He who observes the day, observes it to the Lord; and he who does not observe the day, to the Lord he does not observe it. He who eats, eats to the Lord, for he gives God thanks; and he who does not eat, to the Lord he does not eat, and gives God thanks. For none of us lives to himself, and no one dies to himself. For if we live, we live to the Lord; and if we die, we die to the Lord. Therefore, whether we live or die, we are the Lord's. For to this end Christ died and rose and lived again, that He might be Lord of both the dead and the living. But why do you judge your brother? Or why do you show contempt for your brother? For we shall all stand before the judgment seat of Christ. For it is written:

"As I live, says the LORD,
Every knee shall bow to Me,
And every tongue shall confess to God."

So then each of us shall give account of himself to God. Therefore let us not judge one another anymore, but rather resolve this, not to put a stumbling block or a cause to fall in our brother's way. (Romans 14:1-13)[12]

Establishing a shared identity is an important part of any process of cooperation and peace. For those of us who understand the importance of balancing our lives, our focus should be on what we have in common with a person rather than what we don't have in common with them. We, as human beings, have too often used race, religion, and politics, to name a few, as categories to divide ourselves rather than looking for the common good that exists between us and letting that good unite us. By focusing on the themes of cooperation and togetherness, we can make a significant contribution towards achieving our own inner peace, as well as breeding more peace into the world. We all should work to cooperate and unify peacefully because in that work itself is peace. In the words of the late Rodney King, "Can't we all get along?"[13]

Finally, all of you be of one mind, having compassion for one another; love as brothers, be tenderhearted, be courteous; not returning evil for evil or reviling for reviling, but on the contrary blessing, knowing that you were called to this, that you may inherit a blessing.

> For "He who would love life
> And see good days,
> Let him refrain his tongue from evil,
> And his lips from speaking deceit.
> Let him turn away from evil and do good;
> Let him seek peace and pursue it.
> For the eyes of the LORD are on the righteous,
> And His ears are open to their prayers;
> But the face of the LORD is against those who do evil."
> (1 Peter 3:8-12)[14]

So many times we hear such statements as "you are either with us or against us." This statement doesn't bring people together, but rather, pushes them further apart. The "Philosophy of Balance" is about peace and understanding the "Art of Compromise." However, let me make myself perfectly clear. Natural order should never be compromised because to do so is to create perversion, perversion is corruption, corruption is wickedness, and wickedness is not of the truth.

At some point, we must be the united people of not only the United States of America, but also of the entire world. This includes Natives, Whites, Blacks, Latinos, Africans, Filipinos, Vietnamese, Cambodians, Malaysians, Chinese, Japanese, Koreans, Indians, Arabs and any other ethnic group that does not wish to identify with the names I listed. I have one love for all regardless of their ethnic background. Let us put on display for all the world to see the beauty of people working together and towards common goals of climate justice, criminal justice, racial justice, immigrant rights, religious rights, human rights, and women's rights, as we all come together as one.

In the United States, we must identify with what it is and not with what it was. It is some of this and some of that, a little bit of this and a little bit of that, all mixed together in one big pot; it's gumbo, people! And we would do far better to identify with the stew, rather than with the separate ingredients of the stew. It would be very helpful if people would stop barricading themselves in their own ideological silos. The bottom line is this; together we are better and we must work together to bring the circle of life into balance.

Let me make myself perfectly clear. It is Satan who is the ringleader of rebellion. It is Satan who is against all righteous order, laws, and cooperation that elevate the common good of mankind. It is Satin who wishes to divide and rule, but let us (mankind) not allow that authority to ever come over us. Now is the time, people, to put your right hand on your left shoulder and your left hand on your right shoulder and send out a love hug to the world.

"Me only have one ambition, y' know. I only have one thing I really like to see happen. I like to see mankind live together – black, white, Chinese, everyone – that's all." – Bob Marley[15]

"We must learn to live together as brothers or perish together as fools." – Dr. Martin Luther King Jr.[16]

Competition

: the act or process of competing
: rivalry, a contest between rivals
: one's competitors[1]

Competition is the critical driver of strength, innovation, and performance, but it is not always about getting ahead of others or winning a race, which is more synonymous with envy, greed, and narcissism. However, we must understand that we all have competitive feelings and that they are natural and unavoidable.

It's very important to know how to embrace your competitiveness in a healthy way because competitive feelings do not discriminate. They can be felt towards a total stranger, a co-worker, a friend or even a sibling. Competitive thoughts and feelings must be managed, and the most important thing you must realize about managing your thoughts and feelings is that they are separate from actions.

If we realize that our competitive thoughts and feelings are negative, then we need to make sure the negative thoughts and feelings are not allowed to manifest into negative actions. We will not always have the right thoughts and feelings. However, a wise person learns to correct their thoughts, begins to feel positive, and gains the courage to do the right thing. Wherever thoughts go, energy flows, so do your best to make sure that your information and thoughts propel you positively rather than negatively.

Learn to be diligent and competitive in a righteous way. It's a lot easier to pass on a story than to fact check it, but the latter is more honorable. Facts are our friends. The news should inform us, not affirm us. He that is diligent towards the facts will find the truth.

"Be strong and of good courage, do not fear nor be afraid of them; for the LORD your God, He is the One who goes with you. He will not leave you nor forsake you." (Deuteronomy 31:6)[2]

"Be diligent to present yourself approved to God, a worker who does not need to be ashamed, rightly dividing the word of truth." (2 Timothy 2:15)[3]

Competition is a good thing when it is just and fair. But when the wealthiest one percent has owned more wealth than the rest of the planet since 2015 then something is unfair.[4] First and foremost, the wealthiest people and large corporations should each pay more taxes. Second, billionaires and wealthy campaign contributors should not be the ones determining what is happening in Washington, D.C. Fair and just competition must be a part of the political process for us to truly strive towards unification as a people. An unlevel playing field is not the righteous way to move forward.

In November of 2014, more than sixty-three percent of Americans did not vote in the elections. Approximately eighty percent of voters between the ages of eighteen and twenty-nine also did not vote. This is the lowest voter turnout in seventy years dating all the way back to World War II.[5] Far too many Americans did not allow their voice to count because they never took the time to step up and compete. All American citizens that are eighteen years old and older need to be involved in the political process because that allows competition to be truly fair.

It is time for a peaceful political revolution. A political revolution will push the revitalization of American democracy, and that revitalization can only be achieved with the highest voter turnout possible.

In the United States of America, the ballot is mightier than the bullet. High voter turnout is what I call "Public Power" and "Public Power" comes from politically conscious people. Political consciousness needs to increase so that political consciousness can become greatly contagious. A great protest is good-trouble, the kind of trouble that demands change and works for the greater good of all people.

Power will concede nothing without a fight. You must fight for freedom in every generation. We need to be thinking about, debating about, and protesting about the important issues, because only then will we have the true political competition that we need in order to make this land a fair and great land for everyone. Competition needs to be in government at every level.

Anti-free-trade? Come on, people; we can't have a closed economy and pretend there's no world out there. We must understand the concept of a global economy. We must understand that there are stages of manufacturing. For example, a car is no longer made in its "country of origin" and then sold from that country to other countries. We have many foreign cars made entirely in the United States. Yes, it is true that we may lose the low wage jobs to other countries, including Mexico. However, that will allow the car companies to sell more cars which allows them to compete with other countries such as Korea and Japan, and in turn, hire more engineers in our country, thus providing us with higher wage jobs that we essentially traded for lower wage jobs. The United States will have the opportunity to get many of the high wage jobs that come out of free trade.

Community colleges and universities are the key building blocks for training and retraining individuals in the United States to provide the majority of the high wage, highly skilled work force this world is in need of. You may be asking what about the low-skilled or single skilled American worker? We need to provide opportunities for retraining for the Americans whose jobs have been eliminated either through technology or through outsourcing. Unfortunately, without opportunities for retraining, those Americans will be working in low-wage servicing jobs. However, there will always be good paying jobs in construction building affordable housing and rebuilding the crumbling infrastructure that exists in our country. These types of jobs will not be outsourced because they can't be outsourced.

The Founding Fathers got it right when they created 3 branches of government (Executive, Legislative and Judicial) to balance power. As American citizens, we must do our part with our vote and make sure that the United States of America doesn't become an oligarchy. It's all about the new economy, not the old economy. Always remember that he or she who graduates at the bottom of his or her class in medical school is still called a doctor. Compete, compete and compete! Competition should be understood, not feared.

"There is nothing to fear but fear itself." – Franklin D. Roosevelt[6]

As I mentioned earlier in the twenty-third chapter of this book (Cooperation), when it comes to students, having a cooperative classroom definitely has its benefits. This book is all about balance and just like a cooperative classroom is beneficial, so also is a competitive classroom. Students need to learn how to mentally and physically compete. In a cooperative classroom, students learn the social skills they need to work together with others, which is a skill they will need throughout their lives in many different contexts. With a competitive classroom, students learn the skills they will need to face the real-world aspects of competition.

Balanced people have both cooperation skills and competition skills. To incorporate both cooperative and competitive classroom teaching strategies into a single classroom requires a balanced approach on the teacher's part, delicately balancing the fine line between cooperation and competition. Teaching in this matter benefits not just the teacher and the students but also the future of our world.

Competition is so important to early learning in life that not allowing a child to participate in a variety of competitive activities, such as youth sports, is to almost neglect the child's early development. Young children are filled with natural energy and transferring that natural energy to competitive activities is extremely beneficial both mentally and physically.

Competitive youth sports like basketball, baseball, football, and soccer, to name a few, can help children to learn important life lessons about strength, teamwork, and the human spirit. Nothing is more powerful than the human spirit, other than the Spirit of the Universe that breathed life into man's nostrils.

"And the LORD God formed man of the dust of the ground, and breathed into his nostrils the breath of life; and man became a living being." (Genesis 2:7)[7]

Participating in sports is a way to teach children to compete in a healthy way, allowing them to gain skills that can be used in all areas of life as they grow older. Playing sports can help children learn how to practice, perform, and improve in order to succeed. Having children participate in sports provides them with the exercise they need to burn calories and helps prevent obesity and diabetes. Furthermore, children who are competitive in sports are motivated to eat healthy while also building self-esteem as they learn to try and succeed at new things.

Competition is something we all need to understand in life. Competition is needed for proper balance. The person who doesn't compete cannot succeed at anything. Nothing in this world is free; everything comes with a price. Pay the price, compete, and get what you need to get. Wrestle and compete, and let the Spirit of the Universe touch you.

Then Jacob was left alone; and a Man wrestled with him until the breaking of day. Now when He saw that He did not prevail against him, He touched the socket of his hip; and the socket of Jacob's hip was out of joint as He wrestled with him. And He said, "Let Me go, for the day breaks." But he said, "I will not let You go unless You bless me!" So He said to him, "What is your name?" He said, "Jacob." And He said, "Your name shall no longer be called Jacob, but Israel; for you have struggled with God and with men, and have prevailed." Then Jacob asked, saying, "Tell me Your name, I pray." And He said, "Why is it that you ask about My name?" And He blessed him there. (Genesis 32:24-29)[8]

It's perfectly fine to struggle and compete. Right fights against wrong all the time. It's fine for people to agree to disagree. There are those who will never agree with me about creation, and I will never agree that evolution disproves creation. No explanation of cosmological processes or biological changes disproves the dependence of all things upon the Spirit of the Universe.

I love the Spirit of the Universe and His righteous balance as well as the liberty of life. But righteousness and liberty often compete against each other in one form or another. We must realize that we must be competitive spiritually. Do not be fooled my brothers and sisters because if your spirit is weak, so too, will be your soul and body. You must have a competitive spirit to truly succeed, so wrestle hard and be a champion in the game of life.

For we do not wrestle against flesh and blood, but against principalities, against powers, against the rulers of the darkness of this age, against spiritual hosts of wickedness in the heavenly places. Therefore take up the whole armor of God, that you may be able to withstand in the evil day, and having done all, to stand. (Ephesians 6:12-13)[9]

Do you not know that those who run in a race all run, but one receives the prize? Run in such a way that you may obtain it. everyone who competes for the prize is temperate in all things. Now they do it to obtain a perishable crown, but we for an imperishable crown. Therefore I run thus: not with uncertainty. Thus I fight: not as one who beats the air. But I discipline my body and bring it into subjection, lest, when I have preached to others, I myself should become disqualified. (1 Corinthians

9:24-27)[10]

Competition is naturally in us and needs to be cultivated and balanced in such a way that allows us to be rich. One important thing to remember; if your mind can conceive it, you can achieve it. If you can see it in your head, you can hold it in your hand.

The "Winning Human Triad" is a concept that explains 3 ways that competitiveness is released: by spiritual power, by psychological toughness, and by physical strength. In other words, the "Winning Human Triad" is the organized effort to use all 3 entities that make up man, to achieve victory. When the "Winning Human Triad" is released success is guaranteed on some level, if not on all levels. This "Winning Human Triad" is also the correct way to love the Spirit of the Universe.

"The LORD our God, the LORD is one! You shall love the LORD your God with all your heart, with all your soul, and with all your strength." (Deuteronomy 6:4-5)[11]

The spirit of man is the best part of man. In your spirit is your power. In the soul of man is everything that you think and everything that you feel, and true toughness can only be tested here. The strength of man is purely physical and can only be measured by the body, in other words, the strength of your physical body.

And you shall remember the LORD your God, for it is He who gives you power to get wealth, that He may establish His covenant which He swore to your fathers, as it is this day. Then it shall be, if you by any means forget the LORD your God, and follow other gods, and serve them and worship them, I testify against you this day that you shall surely perish. As the nations which the LORD destroys before you, so you shall perish, because you would not be obedient to the voice of the LORD your God. (Deuteronomy 8:18-20)[12]

"How hard it is for those who have riches to enter the kingdom of God! For it is easier for a camel to go through the eye of a needle than for a rich man to enter the kingdom of God." (Luke 18:24-25)[13]

In the previous verses, the words riches and rich are referring to wealth. Personal wealth often leads to the rejection of the Spirit of the Universe. If, for whatever reason, you should gain a great deal of power (wealth), you must always remember that power without control is, indeed, very dangerous. So whatever you do, in the event that you should attain such power, strive for balance in order to use your influence in a rich way.

Attraction

: the act, process, or power of attracting: personal charm
: the action or power of drawing forth a response: an attractive
  quality
: something that attracts or is intended to attract people by ap-
  pealing to their desires and tastes[1]

First and foremost, the main thing you need to understand about this chapter is that everything that you want in life, you can attract to yourself. However, the law of attraction does not mean you get what you want; it means you get what you attract. The entire universe, including you and me, is pure energy, differing only in the rate of vibration. Energy cannot be created nor destroyed; it merely changes from one form to another. The characteristic of energy is determined by the specific rate of its vibrations. On the lowest level of vibration is solid matter, which can be seen and touched, and on the highest level of vibration is subtle ether, or spirit.

Attraction is about vibration. For some people the law of attraction is recognizable, and for some people the law of attraction is unrecognizable, but for all people it is simple.

When what you think and what you feel are in agreement with one another, you will attract matching vibrations. But if what you think and what you feel are not in agreement then your vibrations will be confusing.

There are 3 simple and basic steps that need to be applied: ask, seek and knock. However, when you apply these 3 steps, you must apply them with your whole spirit, soul, and body, because only when they are applied in this way will you acquire the true belief that is needed to power the law of attraction. Belief is energy and power. The law of attraction needs to be powered by belief in order to be manifested.

"Ask, and it will be given to you; seek, and you will find; knock, and it will be opened to you. For everyone who asks receives, and he who seeks finds, and to him who knocks it will be opened." (Matthew 7:7-8)[2]

The law of attraction, in so many ways, is all about the seen and unseen energies and vibrations. Every positive and negative thing that has happened to you was attracted by you. The law of attraction is at work every second of the day, and therefore, the need to be understood and balanced is of the utmost importance. Man and woman have a natural attraction for each other. Thought is masculine and emotion is feminine. Both what you think and what you feel is of your soul.

If you have an abundance of positivity in your life, then you clearly understand the law of attraction in a positive manner, either consciously or sub-consciously. Therefore, let's us deal with the negative part of the law of attraction because it is here where the understanding of attraction is more easily taught. However, in this chapter, I will not be dealing with how the law of attraction deals with sickness and death because that is what I call the advanced law of attraction, which I may or may not write about in a future book.

The first thing you must realize is that you were born into this world to experience life fully, and not just the good that it has to offer. How would you appreciate the good if you never experience the bad?

After hard times come easy times and after the rain comes sunshine. Trust me; you will later come to realize that some of your hardest challenges in life would turn out to be some of the best things that could've ever happened to you. In other words, you grow most through your spiritual struggles. Without the right amount of sorrow, suffering, and striving one cannot first attract and then make contact with the Spirit of the Universe in order to live a rich life.

> Who led you through that great and terrible wilderness, in which were fiery serpents and scorpions and thirsty land where there was no water; who brought water for you out of the flinty rock; who fed you in the wilderness with manna, which your fathers did not know, that He might humble you and that He might test you, to do you good in the end. (Deuteronomy 8:15-16)[3]

If negative things are being manifested in your life at an alarming rate, then that means you need to change your vibrations. What you have manifested in your life shows the totality of all your vibrations. The totality of your vibrations always shows a physical manifestation. Your vibrations always leave physical clues. If your vibrations are negative, then there will be a negative physical manifestation. We all have positive and negative vibrations going on in our lives constantly. However, the physical manifestation of your vibrations is the total sum of all vibrations you have impacting your life.

There are 3 ways to change your vibrations outside of what you're thinking. The 3 ways you can change your vibrations are by putting your energy into changing people, changing places and changing things. But you must understand that the law of attraction doesn't have a value system. It does not know if something is good or bad, rather, it gathers like energies together - that's it, plain and simple.

First, let's deal with changing your thinking. Changing your thinking is all about two things. First, stop boarding "Thought Trains" that are going to take you to a negative mental place and second, if by mistake you end up on the wrong "Thought Train," hurry up and get off.

Life is about the people you meet and the things you create with them. When it comes to people, do not acquaint yourself with negative thinking or emotionally unhappy people. To associate with these types of people is a recipe for disaster. The more you are around people who subscribe to this mindset, the greater the chance for your demise. Under these circumstances, the law of attraction will have no choice but to set in on you because of the amount of time you spend with these people.

Humans are susceptible to the thinking and emotions of those with whom they spend the majority of their time. As the old saying goes, "birds of a feather flock together." Emotional states are as infectious as any disease. Sometimes you need to change your people in order to change your vibration to a more positive one. Take the time to understand people and how your interactions with them affect you both positively and negatively.

"When someone shows you who they are, believe them the first time." – Maya Angelou[4]

When it comes to places, being in the wrong place at the wrong time says it all. As the saying goes, if you go to the barbershop enough times, eventually you will get a haircut. You have to be aware of the environments that you frequent. Where you stand physically has everything to do with what you attract physically. You can't get wet if there is no water around you.

How about things? Changing things is not about who you are with or where you are, it's about what you are doing. If you live by the sword, don't be surprised when you die by the sword, because it is much a part of the law of attraction.

"Do not be deceived, God is not mocked; for whatever a man sows, that he will also reap." (Galatians 6:7)[5]

Outside of the Spirit of the Universe, we humans are the most powerful manifesting machines this world will ever know. In order for the law of attraction to work for you for your good, there must be the proper thinking in place. You must participate in the gathering together of a network of like-minded people. You must work on being in the designated place at the designed time. You've got to learn the doing part of doing the right thing. But above all, you must be lined up with the Spirit of the Universe if any attraction, negative or positive, is going to work out for your good.

"And we know that all things work together for good to those who love God, to those who are the called according to His purpose." (Romans 8:28)[6]

Let me make myself perfectly clear. We humans have power, but it is limited. The law of attraction is real, but as in all things, you must understand its power. The power of powers rests with the Spirit of the Universe alone, because all powers are ordained by and subject to the Spirit of the Universe.

"Great is our LORD, and mighty in power; His understanding is infinite." (Psalm 147:5)[7]

And Jesus came and spoke to them, saying, "All authority has been given to Me in heaven and on earth. Go therefore and make disciples of all the nations, baptizing them in the name of the Father and of the Son and of the Holy Spirit, teaching them to observe all things that I have commanded you; and lo, I am with you always, even to the end of the age." Amen. (Matthew 28:18-20)[8]

Yet in all these things we are more than conquerors through Him who loved us. For I am persuaded that neither death nor life, nor angels nor principalities nor powers, nor things present nor things to come, nor height nor depth, nor any other created thing, shall be able to separate us from the love of God which is in Christ Jesus our Lord. (Romans 8:37-39)[9]

He is the image of the invisible God, the firstborn over all creation. For by Him all things were created that are in heaven and that are on earth, visible and invisible, whether thrones or dominions or principalities or powers. All things were created through Him and for Him. And He is before all things, and in Him all things consist. And He is the head of the body, the church, who is the beginning, the firstborn from the dead, that in all things He may have the preeminence. (Colossians 1:15-18)[10]

The way to achieve a positive sum regarding the law of attraction comes by meditation, prayer, faith, and hope. You must rely on the Spirit of the Universe for your power and purpose. Be awake to the Spirit of the Universe and always remember you must be asleep to partake in a dream. Don't let anybody sell you their dream.

But I say to you, my beloved, be awake with faith and hope for your power and your purpose, because it is faith that endures and it is hope that delivers. Beloved, let me make myself perfectly clear; it is very hard to live life without hope, and in fact, it is not natural to do so. You need hope to cope.

The greatest tragedy in life is not death, but rather, a life without purpose. Once you find your power and your purpose, think within the same path as your power and purpose, because it is there you will find your balance.

Find a way to develop a network of people who are on the same "Thought Trains" as you in order to mentally grow and remain mentally strong. Identify the places you need to be physically so that you will be ready and able to capitalize on sudden opportunities. And last, but not least, practice the doing part of doing the right thing.

Love

: strong affection for another arising out of kinship or personalties, such as maternal love for a child

: affection and tenderness felt by lovers

: affection based on admiration, benevolence, or common interests

: an assurance of affection

: warm attachment, enthusiasm, or devotion

: a beloved person, darling

: unselfish loyal and benevolent concern for the good of another

: the fatherly concern of God for humankind

: brotherly concern for others

: a person's adoration of God[1]

Love is the first of the nine attributes of the fruit of the Spirit.

"But the fruit of the Spirit is love, joy, peace, longsuffering, kindness, goodness, faithfulness, gentleness, self-control." (Galatians 5:22-23)[2]

Love is the highest degree of understanding. You will never hear a divorced person honestly say that their past mate was too understanding, nor will you ever find an adult look back at their childhood and complain that their parents were too understanding.

When the degree of understanding is at its highest, it is there you will find love in its purest form. To understand something requires work and to receive the highest degree of understanding is to labor. Therefore, the essence of love is to labor for something and to make that something grow. Love, labor and understanding are inseparable. Love is made stronger by the willingness (labor) to be more understanding.

There is no love without understanding. Love without the proper amount of understanding will wither like a rose without the proper amount of water. The closer we are connected to love, the better connected we are to the Spirit of the Universe.

There are 3 ways to show our love for the Spirit of the Universe: by loving people, by loving the earth and by loving animals. To neglect one is to neglect all.

Jesus answered him, "The first of all the commandments is: 'Hear, O Israel, the LORD our God, the LORD is one. And you shall love the LORD your God with all your heart, with all your soul, with all your mind, and with all your strength.' This is the first commandment. And the second, like it, is this: 'You shall love your neighbor as yourself.' There is no other command-ment greater than these." (Mark 12:29-31)[3]

"Then God said, 'Let Us make man in Our image, according to Our likeness; let them have dominion over the fish of the sea, over the birds of the air, and over the cattle, over all the earth and over every creeping thing that creeps on the earth.'" (Genesis 1:26)[4]

"Then the LORD God took the man and put him in the garden of Eden to tend and keep it." (Genesis 2:15)[5]

The nations were angry, and Your wrath has come,
And the time of the dead, that they should be judged,
And that You should reward

Your servants the prophets and the saints,

And those who fear Your name, small and great,

And should destroy those who destroy the earth. (Revelation 11:18)[6]

"A righteous man regards the life of his animal, but the tender mercies of the wicked are cruel." (Proverbs 12:10)[7]

"Be diligent to know the state of your flocks, and attend to your herds; for riches are not forever, nor does a crown endure to all generations." (Proverbs 27:23-24)[8]

If you give love to your environment, the environment will give you love back. I tell you Beloved, if there are any government agencies that have been put in place by the Spirit of the Universe, one is definitely the Environmental Protection Agency (EPA).

There are 3 types of love. The first and best type of love is called divine-love, which is universal love for everyone and should never be determined by our feelings. Within the totality of divine-love is the love for the Spirit of the Universe and the love for our self. It is the special regard for your own well-being and happiness and has nothing to do with narcissistic characteristics. Before you can love someone else, you must love yourself. Divine-love is more a set of thoughts and behaviors than it is shared experiences.

The second type of love is called develop-love, which can be extended to a relative, mate or friend. It is usually based on shared experiences and develops over time.

The third type of love is called desire-love, which can be described as longing for a romantic and sexual relationship. This desire-love can also be referred to as erotic-love.

No matter what type of love we are talking about, all 3 types live by understanding and die by misunderstanding. Like the rose that is made only of non-rose elements, such as sunlight and water, so too, is love made of only non-love elements, such as compassion and understanding. If we remove the outside elements from the rose, there will be no rose. Likewise, if we remove the outside elements from love, there will be no love. With your compassion and understanding, display your love to all.

> But I say to you who hear: Love your enemies, do good to those who hate you, bless those who curse you, and pray for those who spitefully use you. To him who strikes you on the one cheek, offer the other also. And from him who takes away your cloak, do not withhold your tunic either. Give to everyone who asks of you. And from him who takes away your goods do not ask them back. And just as you want men to do to you, you also do to them likewise. But if you love those who love you, what credit is that to you? For even sinners love those who love them. And if you do good to those who do good to you, what credit is that to you? For even sinners do the same. And if you lend to those from whom you hope to receive back, what credit is that to you? For even sinners lend to sinners to receive as much back. But love your enemies, do good, and lend, hoping for nothing in return; and your reward will be great, and you will be sons of the Most High. For He is kind to the unthankful and evil. Therefore, be merciful, just as your Father also is merciful. (Luke 6:27-36)[9]

When our souls are weak, our compassion and understanding are both limited, and we suffer. We can't tolerate others and their shortcomings. But when our soul is strong, we have enough of both compassion and understanding, and those same things that used to make us suffer, don't make us suffer anymore. When we feed and nourish our soul, our understanding grows. Understanding is the life line to love. If you can't understand, you can't love.

The reason why understanding is the life line to love is that everything is always in a state of change. The main complaint a divorced person would give as their reason for the divorce is that their spouse has changed. If you really want to know the truth, no person and no thing will ever stay the same. Couples who stay in a committed relationship are those couples who adjust and learn how to understand one another's evolving needs.

The same is true with a parent and child relationship. Parents help themselves and their children when they understand their children's emotional and developmental changes as they grow and mature. Remember, the essence of love is to labor for something and to make that something grow. Therefore, we labor for the highest degree of understanding, which is love. It does not matter if it's two adults in a marriage or a parent to child relationship, the love will suffer if there is a breakdown in the understanding.

Love is a learned emotional reaction. Children should first learn love from their parents. Love is also a dynamic interaction. Love is the child of freedom, never that of domination. Most of our understanding and misunderstanding of love is formed early in life. We have to learn how to have understanding and love for ourselves first before we can truly love another. If you believe that you are an accident from some kind of big bang explosion that eventually developed into you, or that you came from an ape or monkey that evolved into you, I can understand why you may not love yourself. But I tell you, it is the love of the Spirit of the Universe that created you, and it is that same love that allows you to love yourself. Love is a common thread that runs through all of creation, but it must be developed. You have to own some love in order to be able to give some love.

One of the most precious inheritances a parent can give a child is the understanding of love. Land, houses, and money may be nice to inherit from our parents, but to inherit from our parents the understanding of love for ourselves and of love for others is truly the first step to becoming well balanced and rich. To live without love in your life is a long, poor life, especially when you consider that the average life expectancy of man is 3 quarters of a hundred years, and four quarters of a hundred years or more may be given, if by reason of strength. In fact, to live to be rich, old and full of days is to see four generations of your children.

"The days of our lives are seventy years; and if by reason of strength they are eighty years." (Psalm 90:10)[10]

"After this Job lived one hundred and forty years, and saw his children and grandchildren for four generations. So Job died, old and full of days." (Job 42:16-17)[11]

The parent is the floor of many first steps in a child's life. Just like the inheritance of understanding love from our parents is precious, so too, is the inheritance of a wife that a man gets from the Spirit of the Universe. A wife signifies love.

"Most men will proclaim each his own goodness, but who can find a faithful man? The righteous man walks in his integrity; His children are blessed after him." (Proverbs 20:6-7)[12]

"He who finds a wife finds a good thing, and obtains favor from the LORD." (Proverbs 18:22)[13]

"Houses and riches are an inheritance from fathers, but a prudent wife is from the LORD." (Proverbs 19:14)[14]

In a deeply understanding and loving marriage between a man and a woman, there is no longer a boundary between the two, but rather, the two become one. When a couple has all 3 types of love in their marriage, it is called supreme-love. With supreme-love, his happiness is her happiness, her sadness is his sadness, and vice versa. When supreme-love is in effect, each person helps to increase the other person's happiness and decrease their sadness. On so many levels, there is no separation, but rather, cooperation and the understanding of being one, which is for the betterment of the world.

"For this reason a man shall leave his father and mother and be joined to his wife, and the two shall become one flesh." (Ephesians 5:31)[15]

One of the things we must be mindful of is when we say "I love you," we often focus more on the "I" and less on the "you," which makes the focus more about how we feel and less on the quality of the "love" that is being offered. It is important we understand that when we say "I love you," the "love" must balance out the "I" and the "you."

Owe no one anything except to love one another, for he who loves another has fulfilled the law. For the commandments, "You shall not commit adultery," "You shall not murder," "You shall not steal," "You shall not bear false witness," "You shall not covet," and if there is any other commandment, are all summed up in this saying, namely, "You shall love your neighbor as yourself." Love does no harm to a neighbor; therefore love is the fulfillment of the law. (Romans 13:8-10)[16]

The works of love boil down to some basic principles. First and foremost, you can only love another when you love yourself. Second, deep listening and kind conversation are essential, so let your ears hear, and your mouth give sound advice, because an empathetic soul is of the utmost importance in achieving the highest degree of understanding, which is love. Last, but not least, always remember, love is an action word.

"My little children, let us not love in word or in tongue, but in deed and in truth." (1 John 3:18)[17]

Though I speak with the tongues of men and of angels, but have not love, I have become sounding brass or a clanging cymbal. And though I have the gift of prophecy, and understand all mysteries and all knowledge, and though I have all faith, so that I could remove mountains, but have not love, I am nothing. And though I bestow all my goods to feed the poor, and though I give my body to be burned, but have not love, it profits me nothing. Love suffers long and is kind; love does not envy; love does not parade itself, is not puffed up; does not behave rudely, does not seek its own, is not provoked, thinks no evil; does not rejoice in iniquity, but rejoices in the truth; bears all things, believes all things, hopes all things, endures all things. Love never fails. But whether there are prophecies, they will fail; whether there are tongues, they will cease; whether there is knowledge, it will vanish away. For we know in part and we prophesy in part. But when that which is perfect has come, then that which is in part will be done away. When I was a child, I spoke as a child, I understood as a child, I thought as a child; but when I became a man, I put away childish things. For now we see in a mirror, dimly, but then face to face. Now I know in part, but then I shall know just as I also am known. And now abide faith, hope, love, these three; but the greatest of these is love. (1 Corinthians 13:1-13)[18]

Let your love be on display in 3 ways: in conduct (actions and temperament), in conversations (words and tone), and in chastity (abstention from wrongful sexual intercourse).

Those who love the Spirit of the Universe are those brothers and sisters who are on the path to mastering and suppressing the wrongful desires and passions of the flesh. Mastering such a task is not easy. Such mastery can only be accomplished by keeping your focus on the Spirit of the Universe, and this I say to you, is a requirement to be able to live and walk in the Spirit. Whether you consider yourself religious or spiritual, the courageous and righteous approach is always down the path of love. I tell you, a parent will run into a burning house to save their child because their love for that child is greater than their fear.

"There is no fear in love; but perfect love casts out fear." (1 John 4:18)[19]

Love has no limits, but sex does.

Sex

: either of the two major forms of individuals that occur in
    many species and that are distinguished respectively as
    female or male especially on the basis of their reproductive
    organs and structures
: sexually motivated phenomena or behavior, sexual intercourse[1]

The basic reason why human beings have sex is that we are pro-
grammed naturally to do so; that's it, simple and plain. The reason
why sex is so much a part of our everyday culture is that sexual desire is not only instinctive, but it is also the strongest desire in man.
That natural, wired-in sex-desire is what promotes species survival.
In other words, human beings, like all other animals, are hardwired
for sex, first and foremost, for the survival of the species. Animals
are born with instincts that guide their behavior. Human beings are
born with instincts as well, but they are also born with the gift of
freewill, which can override their instincts. So while animals may
be having sex instinctively, human beings will be having sex out of
reason. Most people don't understand that sex is a mental exercise
far more than a physical exercise, and that sex can bind as well as
liberate your spirit.

There are 3 reasons why human beings have sex: first for pro-creation, second for pleasure, and third for communication with people. Now the reasons why a person has sex may not happen in the above order, however, those are still the 3 reasons.

What came first the chicken or the egg? The chicken. The Spirit of the Universe is the only One who is all powerful and who is capable of creating something out of nothing, not needing any outside source for creation. The Spirit of the Universe in His infinite power has been known to call man into heaven whole. The Bible states that 3 men ascended spirit, soul, and body into heaven. Enoch was the first, Elijah was the second, and Jesus was the third.

> Enoch lived sixty-five years, and begot Methuselah. After he begot Methuselah, Enoch walked with God three hundred years, and had sons and daughters. So all the days of Enoch were three hundred and sixty-five years. And Enoch walked with God; and he was not, for God took him. (Genesis 5:21-24)[2]

> And so it was, when they had crossed over, that Elijah said to Elisha, "Ask! What may I do for you, before I am taken away from you?" Elisha said, "Please let a double portion of your spirit be upon me." So he said, "You have asked a hard thing. Nevertheless, if you see me when I am taken from you, it shall be so for you; but if not, it shall not be so." Then it happened, as they continued on and talked, that suddenly a chariot of fire appeared with horses of fire, and separated the two of them; and Elijah went up by a whirlwind into heaven. (2 Kings 2:9-11)[3]

> Now when He had spoken these things, while they watched, He was taken up, and a cloud received Him out of their sight. And while they looked steadfastly toward heaven as He went up, behold, two men stood by them in white apparel, who also said, "Men of Galilee, why do you stand gazing up into heaven? This same Jesus, who was taken up from you into heaven, will so come in like manner as you saw Him go into heaven."

(Acts 1:9-11)[4]

There are 3 human beings who were born miraculously. By miraculously, I mean outside of the normal process of human reproduction that the Spirit of the Universe has ordained in which both a man and a woman are required to conceive a child. Adam was created without father or mother. Eve was created from Adam, her husband. Jesus was born of a mother (Mary) but without a father in the traditional sense. The coming together of man and woman is a natural process. Jeremiah is the only person in the Bible who was forbidden to be married by the Spirit of the Universe.

"The word of the LORD also came to me, saying, 'You shall not take a wife, nor shall you have sons or daughters in this place.'" (Jeremiah 16:1-2)[5]

In this chapter, it is important to know the difference between reproduction and procreation, even though they are synonyms. Reproduction is the process by which plants and animals give rise to offspring, thus preserving the species.[6] Procreation is the process that results in begetting or bringing forth offspring.[7]

In today's world, many people are more concerned with the gross national product (GNP) than with the original understanding of creation. Many people are more oriented toward materials than toward morals. Therefore, they associate people more closely with products than with the Spirit of the Universe. This is the reason why so many people have a total disregard for human life.

When a man and woman have sexual intercourse to have babies, it is called procreation. Pro is a prefix that means to advance or project forward. In this case, forward is relating to or concerning the future. Babies are born forward. Creation means coming into being. In other words, we promote the survival of human beings so that we can be in accordance with the mandate of the Spirit of the Universe that we should be fruitful and multiply. When it comes to sex, it is plain to see that the Spirit of the Universe created separate duties for each gender. We, all of mankind, male and female, each have a part - a duty - to play in this world, and we all must understand that order, balance, and peace come from living the way our

Creator designed us to live. Procreation is the number one reason for sex.

> So God created man in His own image; in the image of God He created him; male and female He created them. Then God blessed them, and God said to them, "Be fruitful and multiply; fill the earth and subdue it; have dominion over the fish of the sea, over the birds of the air, and over every living thing that moves on the earth." (Genesis 1:27-28)[8]

The second reason for sex is for pleasure. Sexual pleasure is one of life's most rewarding experiences. Sexual pleasure is the feeling we have when we are sexually aroused. Sexual arousal is our body's response to sexual stimulation. We may become aroused by things we see, hear, smell, taste, or touch. They may happen in the real world, in our imagination, or in our dreams.

Understanding sexual repression is important. Sexual repression is a dangerous state to be in. Nothing inspires murderous mayhem in human beings like sexual repression. When human beings are denied water, food or freedom, they will become desperate and attack what they perceive to be the source of their problem. However, when sexual repression lies within the soul of an individual for too long, the human mind can get twisted to the point of rage in an attempt to fulfill that desire, but rarely does that rage attack the actual source of the repression. Sexual repression is the beginning of the making of the sexual offender, be it a predator, priest or spouse.

All humans have an erogenous zone. An erogenous zone is an area of the human body that has heightened sensitivity and is likely to arouse us when touched. Any place on our skin can be an erogenous zone, and not all of us have the same erogenous zones. We all have different likes and dislikes about where we like to be touched, so our erogenous zones are unique to each of us. For example, our sex organs are very sensitive to touch, but touching other places on our skin can also be arousing. Other erogenous zones may include our ears, necks, nipples, backs, buttocks, legs, and feet, and when a married couple takes the time to understand each other sexually, it is there where the full pleasure of sex lies.

Let me make myself perfectly clear, in the case of a married couple, there is not even so much as a suggestion in the Bible that they should only have sex when they are trying to have children. Also, there is no indication that any copulation occurring between two married people is a sin, in and of its self. There are no restrictions concerning how a married couple may perform or behave in bed. Marriage is an honorable practice and the marriage bed is "undefiled." Therefore, any agreed upon "in-the-bed sexual-act" between only the husband and wife, is free from all guilt, disgrace, shame, sin or laws. The word "undefiled" is used in the bible to describe sinless.

"Marriage is honorable among all, and the bed undefiled; but fornicators and adulterers God will judge." (Hebrews 13:4)[9]

> Nevertheless, because of sexual immorality, let each man have his own wife, and let each woman have her own husband. Let the husband render to his wife the affection due her, and likewise also the wife to her husband. The wife does not have authority over her own body, but the husband does. And likewise the husband does not have authority over his own body, but the wife does. Do not deprive one another except with consent for a time, that you may give yourselves to fasting and prayer; and come together again so that Satan does not tempt you because of your lack of self-control. (1 Corinthians 7:2-5)[10]

The third reason for sex is communication or connection with other people. Human beings are social beings, and so many times, people use sex as a way to communicate with or be connected to other people. Sex, by definition, is one of the purest forms of connection, but it should not be used as the first way to connect with other people. A harlot communicates first in this way. Prostitution is the oldest profession known to man, and at the core of prostitution, is sexual communication and connection. Unfortunately, many people misuse sex by first trying to connect in this way, and this may be the worst reason to have sex. Your sexual partner should be chosen with dignity and respect because through sex you are connected.

> Or do you not know that he who is joined to a harlot is one body with her? For "the two," He says, "shall become one flesh." But he who is joined to the Lord is one spirit with Him. Flee sexual immorality. Every sin that a man does is outside the body, but he who commits sexual immorality sins against his own body. Or do you not know that your body is the temple of the Holy Spirit who is in you, whom you have from God, and you are not your own? For you were bought at a price; therefore glorify God in your body and in your spirit, which are God's. (1 Corinthians 6:16-20)[11]

Person to person contact is a beautiful thing. The truth is, there is no replacement for human touch, and we all need somebody to share that touch connection with. You feel alive when you are close to somebody. The first feeling we develop in the womb is the person to person contact and connection we have with our mother. "Seeing's believing," wrote the 18th century English physician Thomas Fuller, 'but feeling's the truth.'"[12]

Person to person contact is the glue that binds sexual partners. When we think about person to person contact, we think about one person touching another. There are 3 types of touch: vibration, texture, and pressure. During sexual intercourse, all 3 types of touch are in play. For most people, touch is the first feeling we pick up and the last feeling we give up.

Sexual intercourse is all about the physical contact of two people. Without physical contact, there could be no sexual intercourse. Sexual intercourse is a mutual physical and social act between two people. Just a touch of sex can go a long way to the right or to the wrong. Sex is a personal act of deep responsibility.

Sex is man's strongest desire, a major source of action, and when that same desire is pressed into creative energy, creativity comes forward. Without sexual desire, man has very little energy for creativity. This fact applies to man and animal, and one only needs to consider the actions of a castrated man, bull or dog as evidence. Their energy is low, and they often become docile, overweight and submissive.

When sexual desire is harnessed and transmuted into creative energy, this transmutation is akin to taming the beast. And when such energy is properly directed toward a target, such a target will have very little chance of not being hit.

Sex is a physical need for most people, but like all needs in life, it must be balanced. Sex should not live alone and should always be balanced by love. Men who partake in sex without love are at risk of developing satyriasis. Women who partake in sex without love are at risk of becoming a nymphomaniac.

One must beware of the fact that alcohol and sex can become dangerous and unbalanced partners in life. Alcohol has been known to promote sexual desire, both wanted as well as unwanted. And although alcohol has been known to promote sexual desire, it has also been known to prevent sexual performance.

Sex without love is a wasteful and self-destructive force and many people have fallen to ruin because their sexual conduct lacked love, which is why sex must not live without love. Achieving balance in sexual affairs promotes spiritual peace. It is the perfect godly form of male dominance and female submission, which is clean and holy. Like food needs drink, sex needs love.

When it comes to sex, the man is fire and the woman is water. The man is hot without woman and the woman is cold without man. When in proper balance, such as during sexual intercourse within a loving relationship, the fire will not dry the water up, and the water will not put out the fire. Thus the hot fire and the cold water both become warm bliss. It is the successful coming together of the two halves. However, when the foundation of a relationship is lust, either the water will extinguish the fire, or the fire will dry the water up. There must be love to balance the two. Balance is nature's way. A sexual affair without love will eventually collapse. Sex should enrich your life, not debase your life.

> For this reason God gave them up to vile passions. For even their women exchanged the natural use for what is against nature. Likewise also the men, leaving the natural use of the woman, burned in their lust for one another, men with men committing what is shameful, and receiving in themselves the penalty of their error which was due. And even as they did not like to retain God in their knowledge, God gave them over to a debased mind, to do those things which are not fitting; being filled with all unrighteousness, sexual immorality, wickedness, covetousness, maliciousness; full of envy, murder, strife, deceit, evil-mindedness; they are whisperers, backbiters, haters of God, violent, proud, boasters, inventors of evil things, disobedient to parents, undiscerning, untrustworthy, unloving, unforgiving, unmerciful; who, knowing the righteous judgment of God, that those who practice such things are deserving of death, not only do the same but also approve of those who practice them. (Romans 1:26-32)[13]

> Drink water from your own cistern,
> And running water from your own well.
> Should your fountains be dispersed abroad,
> Streams of water in the streets?
> Let them be only your own,
> And not for strangers with you.
> Let your fountain be blessed,
> And rejoice with the wife of your youth.
> As a loving deer and a graceful doe,
> Let her breasts satisfy you at all times;
> And always be enraptured with her love.
> For why should you, my son,
> Be enraptured by an immoral woman,
> And be embraced in the arms of a seductress?

(Proverbs 5:15-20)[14]

Once again, it is important for us to realize that sexual desire is a feeling that the Spirit of the Universe has put in human beings for the continuation of the generations. The Spirit of the Universe also has put pleasure in sexual desire, because if there was no pleasure in sexual desire, then many people would not live up to the responsibilities of marriage, giving birth, and raising a child, so that the generations could continue in an orderly fashion.

Sexual intercourse is much more than a consensual physical act between two individuals; it is an act of great responsibility and pleasure. There are 3 things that every person should hope to do before dying: enjoy a spouse, raise a child and kiss a grandchild. All 3 are naturally connected to the responsibilities and pleasures that sexual intercourse brings. However, people must also control the sexual desire that lies in them, or that desire will become dominating and bring them pain instead of pleasure.

Remember, love has no limits, but sex does.

Two are better than one,
Because they have a good reward for their labor.
For if they fall, one will lift up his companion.
But woe to him who is alone when he falls,
For he has no one to help him up.
Again, if two lie down together, they will keep warm;
But how can one be warm alone?
Though one may be overpowered by another,
Two can withstand him.
And a threefold cord is not quickly broken.
(Ecclesiastes 4:9-12)[14]

"Therefore if you have not been faithful in the unrighteous mammon, who will commit to your trust the true riches?"
          – *Jesus Christ*[15]

I have nothing new to teach the world. There is nothing older than God and His power. All that I hope to do is to balance and bear witness to them both in a rich way.

Love Love, Hate, Hate.
May the Spirit be with you.

R. R. Bennett, Sr.

Life Enrichment Coach

References

Title Pages

1. For though I am free from all men, I have made myself a servant to all, that I might win the more; and to the Jews I became as a Jew, that I might win Jews; to those who are under the law, as under the law, that I might win those who are under the law; to those who are without law, as without law (not being without law toward God, but under law toward Christ), that I might win those who are without law; to the weak I became as weak, that I might win the weak. I have become all things to all men, that I might by all means save some. Now this I do for the gospel's sake, that I may be partaker of it with you. - Apostle Paul (1 Corinthians 9:19-23)

Introduction

1. Honest weights and scales are the LORD's; All the weights in the bag are His work. (Proverbs 16:11)

Chapter 1 – Man

1. "Definition of Man," Merriam-Webster Dictionary, accessed on October 13, 2015, http://www.merriam-webster.com/dictionary/man.

2. And the LORD God formed man of the dust of the ground, and breathed into his nostrils the breath of life; and man became a living being. (Genesis 2:7)

3. Let us hear the conclusion of the whole matter: Fear God and keep His commandments, For this is man's all. (Ecclesiastes 12:13)

4. Now in the morning, having risen a long while before daylight, He went out and departed to a solitary place; and there He prayed. (Mark 1:35)

5. But I want you to know that the head of every man is Christ, the head of woman is man, and the head of Christ is God. (1 Corinthians 11:3)

6. Watch, stand fast in the faith, be brave, be strong. Let all that you do be done with love. (1 Corinthians 16:13-14)

7. But the fruit of the Spirit is love, joy, peace, longsuffering, kindness, goodness, faithfulness, gentleness, self-control. Against such there is no law. And those who are Christ's have crucified the flesh with its passions and desires. If we live in the Spirit, let us also walk in the Spirit. (Galatians 5:22-25)

8. Have you not read that He who made them at the beginning, "made them male and female," and said, "For this reason a man shall leave his father and mother and be joined to his wife, and the two shall become one flesh?" So then, they are no longer two but one flesh. Therefore what God has joined together, let not man separate. (Matthew 19:4-6)

9. He who finds a wife finds a good thing, And obtains favor from the LORD. (Proverbs 18:22)

10. Husbands, love your wives, just as Christ also loved the church and gave Himself for her, that He might sanctify and cleanse her with the washing of water by the word, that He might present her to Himself a glorious church, not having spot or wrinkle or any such thing, but that she should be holy and without blemish. So husbands ought to love their own wives as their own bodies; he who loves his wife loves himself. For no one ever hated his own flesh, but nourishes and cherishes it, just as the Lord does the church. For we are members of His body, of His flesh and of His bones. "For this reason a man shall leave his father and mother and be joined to his wife, and the two shall become one flesh." This is a great mystery, but I speak concerning Christ and the church. Nevertheless let each one of you in particular so love his own wife as himself, and let the wife see that she respects her husband. (Ephesians 5:25-33)

11. Better to dwell in a corner of a housetop, than in a house shared with a contentious woman. (Proverbs 21:9)

12. When I was a child, I spoke as a child, I understood as a child, I thought as a child; but when I became a man, I put away childish things. (1 Corinthians 13:11)

13. But now you yourselves are to put off all these: anger, wrath, malice, blasphemy, filthy language out of your mouth. Do not lie to one another, since you have put off the old man with his deeds, and have put on the new man who is renewed in knowledge according to the image of Him who created him. (Colossians 3:8-10)

14. "Physical Difference Between Men and Women," One Talk, accessed on June 26, 2016, http://www.oneplace.com/ministries/family-talk/read/articles/physical-differences-between-men-and-women-15008.html.

15. And God spoke all these words, saying: I am the LORD your God, who brought you out of the land of Egypt, out of the house of bondage.
You shall have no other gods before Me.
You shall not make for yourself a carved image—any likeness of anything that is in heaven above, or that is in the earth beneath, or that is in the water under the earth; you shall not bow down to them nor serve them. For I, the LORD your God, am a jealous God, visiting the iniquity of the fathers upon the children to the third and fourth generations of those who hate Me, but showing mercy to thousands, to those who love Me and keep My commandments.
You shall not take the name of the LORD your God in vain, for the LORD will not hold him guiltless who takes His name in vain.
Remember the Sabbath day, to keep it holy. Six days you shall labor and do all your work, but the seventh day is the Sabbath of the LORD your God. In it you shall do no work: you, nor your son, nor your daughter, nor your male servant, nor your female servant, nor your cattle, nor your stranger who is within your gates. For in six days the LORD made the heavens and the earth, the sea, and all that is in them, and rested the seventh day. Therefore the LORD blessed the Sabbath day and hallowed it.
Honor your father and your mother, that your days may be long upon the land which the LORD your God is giving you.
You shall not murder.
You shall not commit adultery.
You shall not steal.
You shall not bear false witness against your neighbor.
You shall not covet your neighbor's house; you shall not covet your neighbor's wife, nor his male servant, nor his female servant, nor his ox, nor his donkey, nor

anything that is your neighbor's. (Exodus 20:1-17)

16. As long as my breath is in me,
And the breath of God in my nostrils,
My lips will not speak wickedness,
Nor my tongue utter deceit.
Far be it from me
That I should say you are right;
Till I die I will not put away my integrity from me.
My righteousness I hold fast, and will not let it go;
My heart shall not reproach me as long as I live. (Job 27:3-6)

17. You shall do no injustice in judgment, in measurement of length, weight, or volume. You shall have honest scales, honest weights, an honest ephah, and an honest hin. (Leviticus 19:35-36)

18. Let me be weighed on honest scales, that God may know my integrity. (Job 31:6)

19. Dishonest scales are an abomination to the LORD, but a just weight is His delight. (Proverbs 11:1)

20. All things are lawful for me, but all things are not helpful. All things are lawful for me, but I will not be brought under the power of any. (1 Corinthians 6:12)

Chapter 2 – Woman

1. "Definition of Woman," Merriam-Webster Dictionary, accessed on October 13, 2015, http://www.merriam-webster.com/dictionary/women.

2. And the LORD God caused a deep sleep to fall on Adam, and he slept; and He took one of his ribs, and closed up the flesh in its place. Then the rib which the LORD God had taken from man He made into a woman, and He brought her to the man. And Adam said:
"This is now bone of my bones
And flesh of my flesh;
She shall be called Woman,
Because she was taken out of Man."
Therefore a man shall leave his father and mother and be joined to his wife, and

they shall become one flesh. And they were both naked, the man and his wife, and were not ashamed. (Genesis 2:21-25)

3. To the woman He said:
"I will greatly multiply your sorrow and your conception;
In pain you shall bring forth children;
Your desire shall be for your husband,
And he shall rule over you." (Genesis 3:16)

4. An excellent wife is the crown of her husband, but she who causes shame is like rottenness in his bones. (Proverbs 12:4)

5. She opens her mouth with wisdom,
And on her tongue is the law of kindness.
She watches over the ways of her household,
And does not eat the bread of idleness.
Her children rise up and call her blessed;
Her husband also, and he praises her:
"Many daughters have done well,
But you excel them all."
Charm is deceitful and beauty is passing,
But a woman who fears the LORD, she shall be praised.
Give her of the fruit of her hands,
And let her own works praise her in the gates. (Proverbs 31:26-31)

6. The older women likewise, that they be reverent in behavior, not slanderers, not given to much wine, teachers of good things - that they admonish the young women to love their husbands, to love their children, to be discreet, chaste, homemakers, good, obedient to their own husbands, that the word of God may not be blasphemed. (Titus 2:3-5)

7. Now when the queen of Sheba heard of the fame of Solomon concerning the name of the LORD, she came to test him with hard questions. She came to Jerusalem with a very great retinue, with camels that bore spices, very much gold, and precious stones; and when she came to Solomon, she spoke with him about all that was in her heart. So Solomon answered all her questions; there was nothing so difficult for the king that he could not explain it to her. And when the queen of Sheba had seen all the wisdom of Solomon, the house that he had built, the food on his table, the seating of his servants, the service of his

waiters and their apparel, his cupbearers, and his entryway by which he went up to the house of the LORD, there was no more spirit in her. Then she said to the king: "It was a true report which I heard in my own land about your words and your wisdom. However I did not believe the words until I came and saw with my own eyes; and indeed the half was not told me. Your wisdom and prosperity exceed the fame of which I heard. Happy are your men and happy are these your servants, who stand continually before you and hear your wisdom! Blessed be the LORD your God, who delighted in you, setting you on the throne of Israel! Because the LORD has loved Israel forever, therefore He made you king, to do justice and righteousness." (1 Kings 10:1-9)

8. "Women of Ancient Egypt," Ancient Civilizations, accessed on July 4, 2016, http://www.ushistory.org/civ/3f.asp.

Chapter 3 – Child

1. "Definition of Child," Merriam-Webster Dictionary, accessed on October 13, 2015, http://www.merriam-webster.com/dictionary/child.

2. And these words which I command you today shall be in your heart. You shall teach them diligently to your children, and shall talk of them when you sit in your house, when you walk by the way, when you lie down, and when you rise up. You shall bind them as a sign on your hand, and they shall be as frontlets between your eyes. You shall write them on the doorposts of your house and on your gates. (Deuteronomy 6:6-9)

3. Children, obey your parents in the Lord, for this is right. "Honor your father and mother," which is the first commandment with promise: "that it may be well with you and you may live long on the earth." And you, fathers, do not provoke your children to wrath, but bring them up in the training and admonition of the Lord. (Ephesians 6:1-4)

4. From a letter written in 1855 by Frederick Douglass, accessed on July 5, 2016, http://www.deseretnews.com/top/3042/6/The-strength-of-family-16-Frederick-Douglass-quotes.html.

5. He who spares his rod hates his son, but he who loves him disciplines him promptly. (Proverbs 13:24)

6.   Foolishness is bound up in the heart of a child; the rod of correction will drive it far from him. (Proverbs 22:15)

7.   Do not withhold correction from a child, for if you beat him with a rod, he will not die. (Proverbs 23:13)

8.   You shall beat him with a rod, and deliver his soul from hell. (Proverbs 23:14)

9.   Then the king answered the people roughly, and rejected the advice which the elders had given him; and he spoke to them according to the advice of the young men, saying, "My father made your yoke heavy, but I will add to your yoke; my father chastised you with whips, but I will chastise you with scourges!" (1 Kings 12:13-14)

10. Then King Rehoboam consulted the elders who stood before his father Solomon while he still lived, saying, "How do you advise me to answer these people?" And they spoke to him, saying, "If you are kind to these people, and please them, and speak good words to them, they will be your servants forever." But he rejected the advice which the elders had given him, and consulted the young men who had grown up with him, who stood before him. And he said to them, "What advice do you give? How should we answer this people who have spoken to me, saying, 'Lighten the yoke which your father put on us'?" Then the young men who had grown up with him spoke to him, saying, "Thus you should speak to the people who have spoken to you, saying, 'Your father made our yoke heavy, but you make it lighter on us'—thus you shall say to them: 'My little finger shall be thicker than my father's waist! And now, whereas my father put a heavy yoke on you, I will add to your yoke; my father chastised you with whips, but I will chastise you with scourges!'" (2 Chronicles 10:6-11)

Chapter 4 – Water

1.   "Definition of Water," Merriam-Webster Dictionary, accessed on October 13, 2015, http://www.merriam-webster.com/dictionary/water.

2.   "The Water in You: What Does Water Do For You? The USGS Water Science School, accessed on July 19, 2016, http://water.usgs.gov/edu/propertyyou.html.

3.   Jesus answered, "Most assuredly, I say to you, unless one is born of water and

the Spirit, he cannot enter the kingdom of God." (John 3:5)

4. "6 Reasons to Drink Water," page 1, WebMD, accessed on August 1, 2016, http://www.webmd.com/diet/features/6-reasons-to-drink-water?page=1#1.

5. "6 Reasons to Drink Water," page 3, WebMD, accessed on August 1, 2016, http://www.webmd.com/diet/features/6-reasons-to-drink-water?page=1#3.

6. "6 Reasons to Drink Water," page 2, WebMD, accessed on August 8, 2016, http://www.webmd.com/diet/features/6-reasons-to-drink-water?page=1#2.

7. "Negative Ions," Team Ionic, accessed on August 10, 2016, http://www.ionic-balance.com/technology/what-are-negative-ions.

8. "Negative Ions Create Positive Vibes," WebMD, accessed on August 12, 2016, http://www.webmd.com/balance/features/negative-ions-create-positive-vibes?page=2.

9. Howard, Pierce J. Ph.D., The Owner's Manual for the Brain: Everyday Applications from Mind-Brain Research. Austin: Bard Press, 2006.

10. "What are Negative and Positive Ions?" Negative Ionizers, accessed on August 12, 2016, http://negativeionizers.net/negative-and-positive-ions/.

11. "The Water Crisis," Water.org, accessed on August 14, 2016, http://water.org/water-crisis/water-sanitation-facts/.

12. Then God said, "Let the waters abound with an abundance of living creatures, and let birds fly above the earth across the face of the firmament of the heavens." So God created great sea creatures and every living thing that moves, with which the waters abounded, according to their kind, and every winged bird according to its kind. And God saw that it was good. And God blessed them, saying, "Be fruitful and multiply, and fill the waters in the seas, and let birds multiply on the earth." (Genesis 1:20-22)

13. For as the rain comes down,
And the snow from heaven,
And do not return there,
But water the earth,

And make it bring forth and bud,

That it may give seed to the sower

And bread to the eater,

So shall My word be that goes forth from My mouth;

It shall not return to Me void,

But it shall accomplish what I please,

And it shall prosper in the thing for which I sent it. (Isaiah 55:10-11)

14. Let us know,

Let us pursue the knowledge of the LORD.

His going forth is established as the morning;

He will come to us like the rain,

Like the latter and former rain to the earth. (Hosea 6:3)

15. But let justice run down like water, and righteousness like a mighty stream. (Amos 5:24)

16. Who then is Paul, and who is Apollos, but ministers through whom you believed, as the Lord gave to each one? I planted, Apollos watered, but God gave the increase. So then neither he who plants is anything, nor he who waters, but God who gives the increase. Now he who plants and he who waters are one, and each one will receive his own reward according to his own labor. (1 Corinthians 3:5-8)

17. Then I will sprinkle clean water on you, and you shall be clean; I will cleanse you from all your filthiness and from all your idols. I will give you a new heart and put a new spirit within you; I will take the heart of stone out of your flesh and give you a heart of flesh. I will put My Spirit within you and cause you to walk in My statutes, and you will keep My judgments and do them. (Ezekiel 36:25)

18. Let us draw near with a true heart in full assurance of faith, having our hearts sprinkled from an evil conscience and our bodies washed with pure water. (Hebrews 10:22)

Chapter 5 – Air

1. "Definition of Air," Merriam-Webster Dictionary, accessed on October 13, 2015, http://www.merriam-webster.com/dictionary/air.

2. The Spirit of God has made me, and the breath of the Almighty gives me life. (Job 33:4)

3. You hide Your face, they are troubled; You take away their breath, they die and return to their dust. (Psalm 104:29)

4. "FACTS: Danger in the Air – Air Pollution and Cardiovascular Disease," American Heart Association, accessed July 20, 2017, https://www.heart.org/idc/groups/heart-public/@wcm/@adv/documents/downloadable/ucm_463344.pdf.

5. "Smog in our brains," American Psychological Association, accessed on August 30, 2016, http://www.apa.org/monitor/2012/07-08/smog.aspx.

6. "The Terrifying Truth About Air Pollution and Dementia," Mother Jones, accessed on August 30, 2016, http://www.motherjones.com/environment/2015/05/air-pollution-dementia-alzheimers-brain.

7. Thus says God the LORD,
Who created the heavens and stretched them out,
Who spread forth the earth and that which comes from it,
Who gives breath to the people on it,
And spirit to those who walk on it. (Isaiah 42:5)

8. "Particle Pollution," American Lung Association, accessed on September 5, 2016, http://www.lung.org/our-initiatives/healthy-air/outdoor/air-pollution/particle-pollution.html.

9. "Top 22 Benefits of Trees," Tree People, accessed on September 8, 2016, https://www.treepeople.org/resources/tree-benefits.

10. "Benefits of Trees," Arbor Day Foundation, accessed on September 8, 2016, https://www.arborday.org/trees/benefits.cfm.

Chapter 6 – Land

1. "Definition of Land," Merriam-Webster Dictionary, accessed on October 13, 2015, http://www.merriam-webster.com/dictionary/land.

2. "Are There Oceans on Other Planets?" National Ocean Service, accessed on September 23, 2016, http://oceanservice.noaa.gov/facts/et-oceans.html.

3. It is He who sits above the circle of the earth. (Isaiah 40:22)

4. In the beginning God created the heavens and the earth. (Genesis 1:1)

5. And God called the dry land Earth, and the gathering together of the waters He called Seas. And God saw that it was good. (Genesis 1:10)

6. One generation passes away, and another generation comes; but the earth abides forever. (Ecclesiastes 1:4)

7. "What is an Atom?" Life Science, accessed on July 20, 2017, http://www.livescience.com/37206-atom-definition.html.

8. This is the history of the heavens and the earth when they were created, in the day that the LORD God made the earth and the heavens, before any plant of the field was in the earth and before any herb of the field had grown. For the LORD God had not caused it to rain on the earth, and there was no man to till the ground; but a mist went up from the earth and watered the whole face of the ground. And the LORD God formed man of the dust of the ground, and breathed into his nostrils the breath of life; and man became a living being. (Genesis 2:4-7)

9. For He knows our frame; He remembers that we are dust. (Psalm 103:14)

10. I said, "You are gods, And all of you are children of the Most High." (Psalm 82:6)

11. Jesus answered them, "Is it not written in your law, 'I said, "You are gods"'?" (John 10:34)

12. The heaven, even the heavens, are the LORD's; but the earth He has given to the children of men. (Psalm 115:16)

13. I have made the earth, the man and the beast that are on the ground, by My great power and by My outstretched arm, and have given it to whom it seemed proper to Me. (Jeremiah 27:5)

14. For thus says the LORD,
Who created the heavens,
Who is God,
Who formed the earth and made it,
Who has established it,
Who did not create it in vain,
Who formed it to be inhabited:
"I am the LORD, and there is no other." (Isaiah 45:18)

15. "Soil Health: Healthy Soil for Life," Natural Resources Conservation Services, Soils, United States Department of Agriculture, accessed on June 26, 2016, http://www.nrcs.usda.gov/wps/portal/nrcs/main/soils/health/.

16. "Definition of Humus," Merriam-Webster Dictionary, accessed on October 6, 2016, http://www.merriam-webster.com/dictionary/humus.

17. "Soil Organic Matter," Cornell University Cooperative Extension, accessed on June 27, 2016, http://nmsp.cals.cornell.edu/publications/factsheets/factsheet41.pdf.

18. "Soil Quality," Penn State Extension, accessed on June 27, 2016, http://extension.psu.edu/business/start-farming/soils-and-soil-management/soil-quality-introduction-to-soils-fact-sheet.

19. Then another of His disciples said to Him, "Lord, let me first go and bury my father." But Jesus said to him, "Follow Me, and let the dead bury their own dead." (Matthew 8:21-22)

20. "Sensory Receptors," Cliff Notes, accessed on October 13, 2016, https://www.cliffsnotes.com/study-guides/anatomy-and-physiology/the-sensory-system/sensory-receptors.

Chapter 7 – Work

1. "Definition of Work," Merriam-Webster Dictionary, accessed on October 13, 2015, http://www.merriam-webster.com/dictionary/work.

2. "Definition of Sperm," Merriam-Webster Dictionary, accessed October 30, 2016, http://www.merriam-webster.com/dictionary/sperm.

3. In all labor there is profit, but idle chatter leads only to poverty. (Proverbs 14:23)

4. "Dr. Martin Luther King's Economics: Through Jobs, Freedom," The Nation, accessed on July 21, 2017, https://www.thenation.com/article/dr-martin-luther-kings-economics-through-jobs-freedom/.

5. "The Declaration of Independence: A Transcription," American's Founding Documents, National Archives, accessed on July 21, 2017, https://www.archives.gov/founding-docs/declaration-transcript.

6. He who is slothful in his work is a brother to him who is a great destroyer. (Proverbs 18:9)

7. And whatever you do, do it heartily, as to the Lord and not to men, knowing that from the Lord you will receive the reward of the inheritance; for you serve the Lord Christ. (Colossians 3:23-24)

8. What does it profit, my brethren, if someone says he has faith but does not have works? Can faith save him? If a brother or sister is naked and destitute of daily food, and one of you says to them, "Depart in peace, be warmed and filled," but you do not give them the things which are needed for the body, what does it profit? Thus also faith by itself, if it does not have works, is dead. But someone will say, "You have faith, and I have works." Show me your faith without your works, and I will show you my faith by my works. You believe that there is one God. You do well. Even the demons believe—and tremble! But do you want to know, O foolish man, that faith without works is dead? Was not Abraham our father justified by works when he offered Isaac his son on the altar? Do you see that faith was working together with his works, and by works faith was made perfect? And the Scripture was fulfilled which says, "Abraham believed God, and it was accounted to him for righteousness." And he was called the friend of God. You see then that a man is justified by works, and not by faith only. Likewise, was not Rahab the harlot also justified by works when she received the messengers and sent them out another way? For as the body without the spirit is dead, so faith without works is dead also. (James 2:14-26)

9. "Steve Jobs Quotes," Brainy Quote, accessed on December 5, 2016, https://www.brainyquote.com/quotes/authors/s/steve_jobs.html.

Chapter 8 – R & R – Rest and Recreation

1. "Definition of Rest," Merriam-Webster Dictionary, accessed on October 16, 2015, http://www.merriam-webster.com/dictionary/rest.

2. "Definition of Recreation," Merriam-Webster Dictionary, accessed on October 16, 2015, http://www.merriam-webster.com/dictionary/recreation.

3. Thus says the LORD:
"Stand in the ways and see,
And ask for the old paths, where the good way is,
And walk in it;
Then you will find rest for your souls." (Jeremiah 6:16)

4. Thus the heavens and the earth, and all the host of them, were finished. And on the seventh day God ended His work which He had done, and He rested on the seventh day from all His work which He had done. Then God blessed the seventh day and sanctified it, because in it He rested from all His work which God had created and made. (Genesis 2:1-3)

5. Have you not known?
Have you not heard?
The everlasting God, the LORD,
The Creator of the ends of the earth,
Neither faints nor is weary.
His understanding is unsearchable.
He gives power to the weak,
And to those who have no might He increases strength. (Isaiah 40:28-29)

6. My mouth shall speak wisdom, and the meditation of my heart shall give understanding. (Psalm 49:3)

7. Come to Me, all you who labor and are heavy laden, and I will give you rest. Take My yoke upon you and learn from Me, for I am gentle and lowly in heart, and you will find rest for your souls. For My yoke is easy and My burden is light. (Matthew 11:28-30)

8. I know that nothing is better for them than to rejoice, and to do good in their lives, and also that every man should eat and drink and enjoy the good of all his

labor - it is the gift of God. (Ecclesiastes 3:12-13)

Chapter 9 – Sleep

1. "Definition of Sleep," Merriam-Webster Dictionary, accessed on October 15, 2015, https://www.merriam-webster.com/dictionary/sleep.

2. "5 Other Disastrous Accidents Related to Sleep Deprivation," Huffington Post, accessed on November 13, 2016, http://www.huffingtonpost.com/2013/12/03/sleep-deprivation-accidents-disasters_n_4380349.html.

3. "Health Benefits of Napping," Sleep.org, accessed on November 17, 2016, https://sleep.org/articles/napping-health-benefits/.

4. "Melatonin," HOPES – Huntington's Outreach Project for Education, at Stanford, accessed on November 17, 2016, http://web.stanford.edu/group/hopes/cgi-bin/hopes_test/melatonin/.

5. "Melatonin: Extraordinary Antioxidant Benefits Beyond Sleep," BioMedicine.com, accessed on November 23, 2016, http://biomedicine.com/articles/2015/02/03/melatonin-extraordinary-antioxidant-benefits-beyond-sleep.

6. I will both lie down in peace, and sleep; For You alone, O LORD, make me dwell in safety. (Psalms 4:8)

Chapter 10 – Health

1. "Definition of Health," Merriam-Webster Dictionary, accessed on October 15, 2015, http://www.merriam-webster.com/dictionary/health.

2. My son, give attention to my words;
Incline your ear to my sayings.
Do not let them depart from your eyes;
Keep them in the midst of your heart;
For they are life to those who find them
And health to all their flesh. (Proverbs 4:20-22)

3. Beloved, I pray that you may prosper in all things and be in health, just as your soul prospers. (3 John 2)

4. "Constitution of WHO: principles," World Health Organization, accessed on July 25, 2017, http://www.who.int/about/mission/en/.

5. "Anxiety Disorders," National Institute of Mental Health, accessed on November 20, 2016, http://www.nimh.nih.gov/health/topics/anxiety-disorders/index.shtml.

6. "Anxiety Disorders," National Alliance on Mental Illness, accessed on November 20, 2016, https://www.nami.org/Learn-More/Mental-Health-Conditions/Anxiety-Disorders.

7. "Panic Disorders," MentalHealth.gov, accessed on July 26, 2017, https://www.mentalhealth.gov/what-to-look-for/anxiety-disorders/panic-disorder/index.html.

8. "Phobias," Mental Health.gov, accessed on July 26, 2017, https://www.mentalhealth.gov/what-to-look-for/anxiety-disorders/phobias/index.html.

9. "Obsessive-Compulsive Disorder," MentalHealth.gov, accessed on July 26, 2017, https://www.mentalhealth.gov/what-to-look-for/obsessive-compulsive-disorders/index.html.

10. "Post-Traumatic Stress Disorder," MentalHealth.gov, accessed on July 26, 2017, https://www.mentalhealth.gov/what-to-look-for/trauma-stress-related-disorders/index.html.

11. "Depresion," National Alliance on Mental Illness, accessed on November 20, 2016, http://www.nami.org/Learn-More/Mental-Health-Conditions/Depression.

12. "Bipolar Disorder," National Alliance on Mental Illness, accessed on November 20, 2016, http://www.nami.org/Learn-More/Mental-Health-Conditions/Bipolar-Disorder.

13. "Seasonal Affective Disorder," MentalHealth.gov, accessed on November 20, 2016, http://www.mentalhealth.gov/what-to-look-for/mood-disorders/seasonal-affective-disorder/index.html.

Chapter 11 – Wellness

1. "Definition of Wellness," Merriam-Webster Dictionary, accessed on November 10, 2015, https://www.merriam-webster.com/dictionary/wellness.

2. I will praise You, for I am fearfully and wonderfully made; Marvelous are Your works, And that my soul knows very well. (Psalm 139:14)

3. "Health Promotion Glossary Update – New Terms," World Health Organization, accessed on July 26, 2017, http://www.who.int/healthpromotion/about/HPR%20Glossary_New%20Terms.pdf.

4. "About Wellness," National Wellness Institute, accessed on July 26, 2017, http://www.nationalwellness.org/?page=AboutWellness.

Chapter 12 – Sickness

1. "Definition of Sickness," Merriam-Webster Dictionary, accessed on November 12, 2015, http://www.merriam-webster.com/dictionary/sickness.

2. "Your Immune System," Centers for Disease Control and Prevention, accessed on December 5, 2016, http://www.cdc.gov/bam/diseases/immune/immunesys.html.

3. "What are the organs of the immune system," PubMed Health – U.S. National Library of Medicine, accessed on July 27, 2017, http://www.ncbi.nlm.nih.gov/pubmedhealth/PMH0072579/.

4. "The Immune System," University of Rochester Medical Center – Health Encyclopedia, accessed on July 27, 2017, https://www.urmc.rochester.edu/Encyclopedia/Content.aspx?ContentTypeID=90&ContentID=P01665.

5. Is anyone among you sick? Let him call for the elders of the church, and let them pray over him, anointing him with oil in the name of the Lord. And the prayer of faith will save the sick, and the Lord will raise him up. (James 5:14-15)

Chapter 13 – Joy

1. "Definition of Joy," Merriam-Webster Dictionary, accessed on November 16,

2015, http://www.merriam-webster.com/dictionary/joy.

2.   But the fruit of the Spirit is love, joy, peace, longsuffering, kindness, goodness, faithfulness, gentleness, self-control. (Galatians 5:22-23)

3.   As the Father loved Me, I also have loved you; abide in My love. If you keep My commandments, you will abide in My love, just as I have kept My Father's commandments and abide in His love. These things I have spoken to you, that My joy may remain in you, and that your joy may be full. (John 15: 9-11)

4.   Most assuredly, I say to you that you will weep and lament, but the world will rejoice; and you will be sorrowful, but your sorrow will be turned into joy. A woman, when she is in labor, has sorrow because her hour has come; but as soon as she has given birth to the child, she no longer remembers the anguish, for joy that a human being has been born into the world. Therefore you now have sorrow; but I will see you again and your heart will rejoice, and your joy no one will take from you. And in that day you will ask Me nothing. Most assuredly, I say to you, whatever you ask the Father in My name He will give you. Until now you have asked nothing in My name. Ask, and you will receive, that your joy may be full. (John 16:20-24)

5.   Blessed be the LORD,
Because He has heard the voice of my supplications!
The LORD is my strength and my shield;
My heart trusted in Him, and I am helped;
Therefore my heart greatly rejoices,
And with my song I will praise Him. (Psalm 28:6-7)

6.   You will show me the path of life;
In Your presence is fullness of joy;
At Your right hand are pleasures forevermore. (Psalm 16:11)

7.   My brethren, count it all joy when you fall into various trials, knowing that the testing of your faith produces patience. But let patience have its perfect work, that you may be perfect and complete, lacking nothing. (James 1:2-4)

8.   "Transcript: Michelle Obama's DNC Speech," CNN, accessed on July 27, 2017, http://www.cnn.com/2016/07/26/politics/transcript-michelle-obama-speech-democratic-national-convention/.

Chapter 14 – Contentment

1. "Definition of Contentment," Merriam-Webster Dictionary, accessed on December 30, 2016, https://www.merriam-webster.com/dictionary/contentment.

2. Let your conduct be without covetousness; be content with such things as you have. For He Himself has said, "I will never leave you nor forsake you." So we may boldly say: "The LORD is my helper; I will not fear. What can man do to me?" (Hebrew 13:5-6)

3. "Serenity Prayer," PrayerFoundation.org, accessed on November 23, 2015, http://prayerfoundation.org/dailyoffice/serenity_prayer_full_version.htm.

4. He who loves silver will not be satisfied with silver; Nor he who loves abundance, with increase. This also is vanity. (Ecclesiastes 5:10)

5. The LORD is near to those who have a broken heart, And saves such as have a contrite spirit. (Psalm 34:18)

6. And we know that all things work together for good to those who love God, to those who are the called according to His purpose. (Romans 8:28)

7. Not that I speak in regard to need, for I have learned in whatever state I am, to be content: I know how to be abased, and I know how to abound. Everywhere and in all things I have learned both to be full and to be hungry, both to abound and to suffer need. I can do all things through Christ who strengthens me. (Philippians 4:11-13)

Chapter 15 – Pain

1. "Definition of Pain," Merriam-Webster Dictionary, accessed on November 30, 2015, http://www.merriam-webster.com/dictionary/pain.

2. My brethren, be strong in the Lord and in the power of His might. Put on the whole armor of God, that you may be able to stand against the wiles of the devil. For we do not wrestle against flesh and blood, but against principalities, against powers, against the rulers of the darkness of this age, against spiritual hosts of wickedness in the heavenly places. Therefore take up the whole armor of God, that you may be able to withstand in the evil day, and having done all,

to stand. Stand therefore, having girded your waist with truth, having put on the breastplate of righteousness, and having shod your feet with the preparation of the gospel of peace; above all, taking the shield of faith with which you will be able to quench all the fiery darts of the wicked one. And take the helmet of salvation, and the sword of the Spirit, which is the word of God; praying always with all prayer and supplication in the Spirit. (Ephesians 6:10-18)

3. You shall have no other gods before Me. You shall not make for yourself a carved image—any likeness of anything that is in heaven above, or that is in the earth beneath, or that is in the water under the earth; you shall not bow down to them nor serve them. For I, the LORD your God, am a jealous God, visiting the iniquity of the fathers upon the children to the third and fourth generations of those who hate Me, but showing mercy to thousands, to those who love Me and keep My commandments. (Exodus 20:3-6)

4. And He said to me, "My grace is sufficient for you, for My strength is made perfect in weakness." Therefore most gladly I will rather boast in my infirmities, that the power of Christ may rest upon me. Therefore I take pleasure in infirmities, in reproaches, in needs, in persecutions, in distresses, for Christ's sake. For when I am weak, then I am strong. (2 Corinthians 12:9-10)

5. Now no chastening seems to be joyful for the present, but painful; nevertheless, afterward it yields the peaceable fruit of righteousness to those who have been trained by it. (Hebrew 12:11)

6. He is despised and rejected by men, A Man of sorrows and acquainted with grief. (Isaiah 53:3)

7. Be angry, and do not sin: do not let the sun go down on your wrath, nor give place to the devil. (Ephesians 4:26-27)

8. Is there not a time of hard service for man on earth? (Job 7:1)

9. If you endure chastening, God deals with you as with sons; for what son is there whom a father does not chasten? But if you are without chastening, of which all have become partakers, then you are illegitimate and not sons. Furthermore, we have had human fathers who corrected us, and we paid them respect. Shall we not much more readily be in subjection to the Father of spirits and live? (Hebrews 12:7-9)

10. "A. W. Tozer Quotes," Goodreads.com, accessed on January 3, 2017, https://www.goodreads.com/author/quotes/1082290.A_W_Tozer.

Chapter 16 – Food

1. "Definition of Food," Merriam-Webster Dictionary, accessed on December 6, 2015, http://www.merriam-webster.com/dictionary/food.

2. So you shall serve the LORD your God, and He will bless your bread and your water. (Exodus 23:25)

3. "Minerals: What They Do, Where to Get Them," Texas Heart Institute: Heart Information Center, accessed on January 10, 2016, http://www.texasheart.org/HIC/Topics/HSmart/mineral1.cfm.

4. "Trace Minerals: What They Do and Where to Get Them," Texas Heart Institute: Heart Information Center, accessed on January 10, 2016. http://www.texasheart.org/HIC/Topics/HSmart/trace1.cfm.

5. "Why We Need Amino Acids," Health Guidance for Better Health, accessed on January 15, 2017, http://www.healthguidance.org/entry/3454/1/Why-We-Need-Amino-Acids.html.

6. "Seniors – Beef it up to prevent muscle loss," Healthy Lifestyle: Nutrition and Healthy Eating, Mayo Clinic, accessed on January 18, 2017, http://www.mayoclinic.org/healthy-lifestyle/nutrition-and-healthy-eating/expert-blog/seniors-beef-it-up-to-prevent-muscle-loss/bgp-20136508.

7. "How many carbohydrates do you need?" Healthy Lifestyle: Nutrition and Healthy Eating, Mayo Clinic, accessed on January 20, 2017, http://www.mayoclinic.org/healthy-lifestyle/nutrition-and-healthy-eating/in-depth/carbohydrates/art-20045705?pg=2.

8. "Dietary Fats: Know which types to choose," Healthy Lifestyle: Nutrition and Healthy Eating, Mayo Clinic, accessed on January 20, 2017, http://www.mayoclinic.org/healthy-lifestyle/nutrition-and-healthy-eating/in-depth/fat/art-20045550.

9. "Vitamins," Medline Plus: U.S. National Library of Medicine, accessed on

January 20, 2017, https://medlineplus.gov/vitamins.html.

10. And the fear of you and the dread of you shall be on every beast of the earth, on every bird of the air, on all that move on the earth, and on all the fish of the sea. They are given into your hand. Every moving thing that lives shall be food for you. I have given you all things, even as the green herbs. But you shall not eat flesh with its life, that is, its blood. (Genesis 9:2-4)

11. Go, eat your bread with joy, And drink your wine with a merry heart; For God has already accepted your works. (Ecclesiastes 9:7)

12. When He had called all the multitude to Himself, He said to them, "Hear Me, everyone, and understand: There is nothing that enters a man from out-side which can defile him; but the things which come out of him, those are the things that defile a man. If anyone has ears to hear, let him hear!" When He had entered a house away from the crowd, His disciples asked Him concerning the parable. So He said to them, "Are you thus without understanding also? Do you not perceive that whatever enters a man from outside cannot defile him, because it does not enter his heart but his stomach, and is eliminated, thus purifying all foods?" And He said, "What comes out of a man, that defiles a man. For from within, out of the heart of men, proceed evil thoughts, adulteries, fornications, murders, thefts, covetousness, wickedness, deceit, lewdness, an evil eye, blasphe-my, pride, foolishness. All these evil things come from within and defile a man." (Mark 7:14-23)

13. "Mediterranean Diet: A Heart Healthy Eating Plan," Healthy Lifestyle: Nu-trition and Healthy Eating, Mayo Clinic, accessed on December 15, 2016, http://www.mayoclinic.org/healthy-lifestyle/nutrition-and-healthy-eating/in-depth/mediterranean-diet/art-20047801.

14. But food does not commend us to God; for neither if we eat are we the better, nor if we do not eat are we the worse. (1 Corinthians 8:8)

15. Therefore, whether you eat or drink, or whatever you do, do all to the glory of God. Give no offense, either to the Jews or to the Greeks or to the church of God. (1 Corinthians 10:31-32)

Chapter 17 - Shelter

1. "Definition of Shelter," Merriam-Webster Dictionary, accessed on December 9, 2015, http://www.merriam-webster.com/dictionary/shelter.

2. But if anyone does not provide for his own, and especially for those of his household, he has denied the faith and is worse than an unbeliever. (1 Timothy 5:8)

3. Through wisdom a house is built, And by understanding it is established; By knowledge the rooms are filled with all precious and pleasant riches. (Proverbs 24:3-4)

4. My people will dwell in a peaceful habitation, in secure dwellings, and in quiet resting places. (Isaiah 32:18)

5. Now therefore, fear the LORD, serve Him in sincerity and in truth, and put away the gods which your fathers served on the other side of the River and in Egypt. Serve the LORD! And if it seems evil to you to serve the LORD, choose for yourselves this day whom you will serve, whether the gods which your fathers served that were on the other side of the River, or the gods of the Amorites, in whose land you dwell. But as for me and my house, we will serve the LORD. (Joshua 24:14-15)

6. One thing I have desired of the LORD,
That will I seek:
That I may dwell in the house of the LORD
All the days of my life,
To behold the beauty of the LORD,
And to inquire in His temple.
For in the time of trouble
He shall hide me in His pavilion;
In the secret place of His tabernacle
He shall hide me;
He shall set me high upon a rock. (Psalm 27:4-5)

7. And we know that all things work together for good to those who love God, to those who are the called according to His purpose. For whom He foreknew, He also predestined to be conformed to the image of His Son, that He might

be the firstborn among many brethren. Moreover whom He predestined, these He also called; whom He called, these He also justified; and whom He justified, these He also glorified. (Romans 8:28-30)

Chapter 18 - Clothing

1. "Definition of Clothing," Merriam-Webster Dictionary, accessed on December 16, 2015, http://beta.merriam-webster.com/dictionary/clothing.

2. A woman shall not wear anything that pertains to a man, nor shall a man put on a woman's garment, for all who do so are an abomination to the LORD your God. (Deuteronomy 22:5)

3. "Maslow's Hierarchy of Needs," Simply Psychology, accessed on January 23, 2017, http://www.simplypsychology.org/maslow.html.

Chapter 19 - Selfishness

1. "Definition of Selfishness," Merriam-Webster Dictionary, accessed on December 23, 2015, http://www.merriam-webster.com/dictionary/selfish.

2. But let each one examine his own work, and then he will have rejoicing in himself alone, and not in another. For each one shall bear his own load. (Galatians 6:4-5)

3. "Maslow's Hierarchy of Needs," Simply Psychology, accessed on January 23, 2017, http://www.simplypsychology.org/maslow.html.

4. "Carl Rogers," Simply Psychology, accessed on January 28, 2017, http://www.simplypsychology.org/carl-rogers.html#con.

5. Let each of you look out not only for his own interests, but also for the interests of others. (Philippians 2:4)

Chapter 20 - Repentance

1. "Definition of Repent," Merriam-Webster Dictionary, accessed on January 6,

2016, http://www.merriam-webster.com/dictionary/repent.

2. "Steve Jobs Quotes," BrainyQuotes.com, accessed on January 30, 2017, https://www.brainyquote.com/quotes/authors/s/steve_jobs.html.

3. Yet you say, "Why should the son not bear the guilt of the father?" Because the son has done what is lawful and right, and has kept all My statutes and observed them, he shall surely live. The soul who sins shall die. The son shall not bear the guilt of the father, nor the father bear the guilt of the son. The righteousness of the righteous shall be upon himself, and the wickedness of the wicked shall be upon himself. (Ezekiel 18:19-20)

4. But Jesus said, "Let the little children come to Me, and do not forbid them; for of such is the kingdom of heaven." (Matthew 19:14)

5. For all have sinned and fall short of the glory of God. (Romans 3:23)

6. For we do not have a High Priest who cannot sympathize with our weaknesses, but was in all points tempted as we are, yet without sin. (Hebrews 4:15)

7. Who committed no sin, Nor was deceit found in His mouth. (1 Peter 2:22)

8. And you know that He was manifested to take away our sins, and in Him there is no sin. (1 John 3:5)

9. Come to Me, all you who labor and are heavy laden, and I will give you rest. Take My yoke upon you and learn from Me, for I am gentle and lowly in heart, and you will find rest for your souls. For My yoke is easy and My burden is light. (Matthew 11:28-30)

10. He who keeps instruction is in the way of life, But he who refuses correction goes astray. (Proverbs 10:17)

11. If My people who are called by My name will humble themselves, and pray and seek My face, and turn from their wicked ways, then I will hear from heaven, and will forgive their sin and heal their land. (2 Chronicles 7:14)

12. The time is fulfilled, and the kingdom of God is at hand. Repent, and believe in the gospel. (Mark 1:15)

13. Take heed to yourselves. If your brother sins against you, rebuke him; and if he repents, forgive him. And if he sins against you seven times in a day, and seven times in a day returns to you, saying, "I repent," you shall forgive him. (Luke 17:3-4)

14. If we confess our sins, He is faithful and just to forgive us our sins and to cleanse us from all unrighteousness. (1 John 1:9)

15. Therefore, as the elect of God, holy and beloved, put on tender mercies, kindness, humility, meekness, longsuffering; bearing with one another, and forgiving one another, if anyone has a complaint against another; even as Christ forgave you, so you also must do. (Colossians 3:12-13)

16. Do you not know that those who run in a race all run, but one receives the prize? Run in such a way that you may obtain it. And everyone who competes for the prize is temperate in all things. Now they do it to obtain a perishable crown, but we for an imperishable crown. Therefore I run thus: not with uncertainty. Thus I fight: not as one who beats the air. But I discipline my body and bring it into subjection, lest, when I have preached to others, I myself should become disqualified. (1 Corinthians 9:24-27)

17. I have fought the good fight, I have finished the race, I have kept the faith. Finally, there is laid up for me the crown of righteousness, which the Lord, the righteous Judge, will give to me on that Day, and not to me only but also to all who have loved His appearing. (2 Timothy 4:7-8)

18. Then Peter said to them, "Repent, and let every one of you be baptized in the name of Jesus Christ for the remission of sins; and you shall receive the gift of the Holy Spirit. For the promise is to you and to your children, and to all who are afar off, as many as the Lord our God will call." (Acts 2:38-39)

19. Repent therefore and be converted, that your sins may be blotted out, so that times of refreshing may come from the presence of the Lord. (Acts 3:19)

20. When they heard these things they became silent; and they glorified God, saying, "Then God has also granted to the Gentiles repentance to life." (Acts 11:18)

21. Truly, these times of ignorance God overlooked, but now commands all men everywhere to repent. (Acts 17:30)

22. How I kept back nothing that was helpful, but proclaimed it to you, and taught you publicly and from house to house, testifying to Jews, and also to Greeks, repentance toward God and faith toward our Lord Jesus Christ. (Acts 20:20-21)

23. But declared first to those in Damascus and in Jerusalem, and throughout all the region of Judea, and then to the Gentiles, that they should repent, turn to God, and do works befitting repentance. (Acts 26:20)

24. Search me, O God, and know my heart; try me, and know my anxieties; and see if there is any wicked way in me, and lead me in the way everlasting. (Psalm 139:23-24)

25. And we know that all things work together for good to those who love God, to those who are the called according to His purpose. For whom He foreknew, He also predestined to be conformed to the image of His Son, that He might be the firstborn among many brethren. Moreover whom He predestined, these He also called; whom He called, these He also justified; and whom He justified, these He also glorified. (Romans 8:28-30)

26. And those who are Christ's have crucified the flesh with its passions and desires. (Galatians 5:24)

Chapter 21 – Empathy

1. "Definition of Empathy, Merriam-Webster Dictionary, accessed on January 9, 2016, http://www.merriam-webster.com/dictionary/empathy.

2. Therefore, whatever you want men to do to you, do also to them, for this is the Law and the Prophets. (Matthew 7:12)

3. Jesus said to him, "You shall love the Lord your God with all your heart, with all your soul, and with all your mind." This is the first and great commandment. And the second is like it: "You shall love your neighbor as yourself." On these two commandments hang all the Law and the Prophets. (Matthew 22:37-40)

4. Rejoice with those who rejoice, and weep with those who weep. Be of the same mind toward one another. (Romans 12:15-16)

5. Finally, all of you be of one mind, having compassion for one another; love as brothers, be tenderhearted, be courteous; not returning evil for evil or reviling for reviling, but on the contrary blessing, knowing that you were called to this, that you may inherit a blessing.

For "He who would love life
And see good days,
Let him refrain his tongue from evil,
And his lips from speaking deceit.
Let him turn away from evil and do good;
Let him seek peace and pursue it.
For the eyes of the LORD are on the righteous,
And His ears are open to their prayers;
But the face of the LORD is against those who do evil." (1 Peter 3:8-12)

6. So when the woman saw that the tree was good for food, that it was pleasant to the eyes, and a tree desirable to make one wise, she took of its fruit and ate. (Genesis 3:6)

7. Then Jesus, being filled with the Holy Spirit, returned from the Jordan and was led by the Spirit into the wilderness, being tempted for forty days by the devil. And in those days He ate nothing, and afterward, when they had ended, He was hungry. And the devil said to Him, "If You are the Son of God, command this stone to become bread." But Jesus answered him, saying, "It is written, 'Man shall not live by bread alone, but by every word of God.'" Then the devil, taking Him up on a high mountain, showed Him all the kingdoms of the world in a moment of time. And the devil said to Him, "All this authority I will give You, and their glory; for this has been delivered to me, and I give it to whomever I wish. Therefore, if You will worship before me, all will be Yours." And Jesus answered and said to him, "Get behind Me, Satan! For it is written, 'You shall worship the LORD your God, and Him only you shall serve.'" Then he brought Him to Jerusalem, set Him on the pinnacle of the temple, and said to Him, "If You are the Son of God, throw Yourself down from here. For it is written: 'He shall give His angels charge over you, To keep you,' and, 'In their hands they shall bear you up, Lest you dash your foot against a stone.'" And Jesus answered and said to him, "It has been said, 'You shall not tempt the LORD your God.'" Now when the devil had ended every temptation, he departed from Him until an opportune time. (Luke 4:1-13)

Charity – Chapter 22

1. "Definition of Charity," Merriam-Webster Dictionary, accessed on January 13, 2016, http://www.merriam-webster.com/dictionary/charity.

2. "Come, you blessed of My Father, inherit the kingdom prepared for you from the foundation of the world: for I was hungry and you gave Me food; I was thirsty and you gave Me drink; I was a stranger and you took Me in; I was naked and you clothed Me; I was sick and you visited Me; I was in prison and you came to Me." Then the righteous will answer Him, saying, "Lord, when did we see You hungry and feed You, or thirsty and give You drink? When did we see You a stranger and take You in, or naked and clothe You? Or when did we see You sick, or in prison, and come to You?" And the King will answer and say to them, "Assuredly, I say to you, inasmuch as you did it to one of the least of these My brethren, you did it to Me." (Matthew 25:34-40)

3. So now, brethren, I commend you to God and to the word of His grace, which is able to build you up and give you an inheritance among all those who are sanctified. I have coveted no one's silver or gold or apparel. Yes, you yourselves know that these hands have provided for my necessities, and for those who were with me. I have shown you in every way, by laboring like this, that you must support the weak. And remember the words of the Lord Jesus, that He said, "It is more blessed to give than to receive." (Acts 20:32-35)

4. For you know the grace of our Lord Jesus Christ, that though He was rich, yet for your sakes He became poor, that you through His poverty might become rich. (2 Corinthians 8:9)

5. But whoever has this world's goods, and sees his brother in need, and shuts up his heart from him, how does the love of God abide in him? (1 John 3:17)

6. Be hospitable to one another without grumbling. As each one has received a gift, minister it to one another, as good stewards of the manifold grace of God. (1 Peter 4:9-10)

7. If you extend your soul to the hungry and satisfy the afflicted soul, then your light shall dawn in the darkness, and your darkness shall be as the noonday. (Isaiah 58:10)

8. "Be angry, and do not sin:" do not let the sun go down on your wrath, nor give place to the devil. Let him who stole steal no longer, but rather let him labor, working with his hands what is good, that he may have something to give him who has need. Let no corrupt word proceed out of your mouth, but what is good for necessary edification, that it may impart grace to the hearers. And do not grieve the Holy Spirit of God, by whom you were sealed for the day of redemption. Let all bitterness, wrath, anger, clamor, and evil speaking be put away from you, with all malice. And be kind to one another, tenderhearted, forgiving one another, even as God in Christ forgave you. (Ephesians 4:26-32)

9. While they promise them liberty, they themselves are slaves of corruption; for by whom a person is overcome, by him also he is brought into bondage. (2 Peter 2:19)

10. What does it profit, my brethren, if someone says he has faith but does not have works? Can faith save him? If a brother or sister is naked and destitute of daily food, and one of you says to them, "Depart in peace, be warmed and filled," but you do not give them the things which are needed for the body, what does it profit? Thus also faith by itself, if it does not have works, is dead. (James 2:14-17)

11. "Muhammad Ali Quotes," BrainyQuotes.com, accessed on March 4, 2017, https://www.brainyquote.com/quotes/authors/m/muhammad_ali_3.html.

Chapter 23 – Cooperation

1. "Definition of Cooperation," Merriam-Webster Dictionary, accessed on January 23, 2016, http://www.merriam-webster.com/dictionary/cooperation.

2. But the LORD said to Samuel, "Do not look at his appearance or at his physical stature, because I have refused him. For the LORD does not see as man sees; for man looks at the outward appearance, but the LORD looks at the heart." (1 Samuel 16:7)

3. Behold, how good and how pleasant it is for brethren to dwell together in unity! (Psalm 133:1)

4. Be of the same mind toward one another. Do not set your mind on high things, but associate with the humble. (Romans 12:16)

5. "Tarzan the Ape Man," IMDb.com, accessed on March 5, 2017, http://www.imdb.com/title/tt0023551/.

6. "D. W. Griffith's The Birth of a Nation (1915)," The Rise and Fall of Jim Crow, PBS.org, accessed on March 5, 2017, http://www.pbs.org/wnet/jimcrow/stories_events_birth.html.

7. "Great Pyramid: Earth's Largest," Egypt: Secrets of an Ancient World, National Geographic, accessed on March 5, 2017, http://www.nationalgeographic.com/pyramids/khufu.html.

8. "Martin Luther King, Jr. Quotes," BrainyQuotes.com, accessed on March 5, 2017, https://www.brainyquote.com/quotes/authors/m/martin_luther_king_jr.html.

9. "Health Expenditure Per Capita," The World Bank, accessed on March 10, 2107, http://data.worldbank.org/indicator/SH.XPD.PCAP.

10. Do not think that I came to destroy the Law or the Prophets. I did not come to destroy but to fulfill. For assuredly, I say to you, till heaven and earth pass away, one jot or one tittle will by no means pass from the law till all is fulfilled. Whoever therefore breaks one of the least of these commandments, and teaches men so, shall be called least in the kingdom of heaven; but whoever does and teaches them, he shall be called great in the kingdom of heaven. For I say to you, that unless your righteousness exceeds the righteousness of the scribes and Pharisees, you will by no means enter the kingdom of heaven. (Matthew 5:17-20)

11. Now an angel of the Lord spoke to Philip, saying, "Arise and go toward the south along the road which goes down from Jerusalem to Gaza." This is desert. So he arose and went. And behold, a man of Ethiopia, a eunuch of great authority under Candace the queen of the Ethiopians, who had charge of all her treasury, and had come to Jerusalem to worship, was returning. And sitting in his chariot, he was reading Isaiah the prophet. Then the Spirit said to Philip, "Go near and overtake this chariot." So Philip ran to him, and heard him reading the prophet Isaiah, and said, "Do you understand what you are reading?" And he said, "How can I, unless someone guides me?" And he asked Philip to come up and sit with him. The place in the Scripture which he read was this:
"He was led as a sheep to the slaughter;
And as a lamb before its shearer is silent,

So He opened not His mouth.

In His humiliation His justice was taken away,

And who will declare His generation?

For His life is taken from the earth."

So the eunuch answered Philip and said, "I ask you, of whom does the prophet say this, of himself or of some other man?" Then Philip opened his mouth, and beginning at this Scripture, preached Jesus to him. Now as they went down the road, they came to some water. And the eunuch said, "See, here is water. What hinders me from being baptized?" Then Philip said, "If you believe with all your heart, you may." And he answered and said, "I believe that Jesus Christ is the Son of God." So he commanded the chariot to stand still. And both Philip and the eunuch went down into the water, and he baptized him. Now when they came up out of the water, the Spirit of the Lord caught Philip away, so that the eunuch saw him no more; and he went on his way rejoicing. (Acts 8:26-39)

12. Receive one who is weak in the faith, but not to disputes over doubtful things. For one believes he may eat all things, but he who is weak eats only vegetables. Let not him who eats despise him who does not eat, and let not him who does not eat judge him who eats; for God has received him. Who are you to judge another's servant? To his own master he stands or falls. Indeed, he will be made to stand, for God is able to make him stand. One person esteems one day above another; another esteems every day alike. Let each be fully convinced in his own mind. He who observes the day, observes it to the Lord; and he who does not observe the day, to the Lord he does not observe it. He who eats, eats to the Lord, for he gives God thanks; and he who does not eat, to the Lord he does not eat, and gives God thanks. For none of us lives to himself, and no one dies to himself. For if we live, we live to the Lord; and if we die, we die to the Lord. Therefore, whether we live or die, we are the Lord's. For to this end Christ died and rose and lived again, that He might be Lord of both the dead and the living. But why do you judge your brother? Or why do you show contempt for your brother? For we shall all stand before the judgment seat of Christ. For it is written:

"As I live, says the LORD,

Every knee shall bow to Me,

And every tongue shall confess to God."

So then each of us shall give account of himself to God. Therefore let us not judge one another anymore, but rather resolve this, not to put a stumbling block or a cause to fall in our brother's way. (Romans 14:1-13)

13. "Rodney King," Biography.com, accessed on March 10, 2017, http://www.biography.com/people/rodney-king-9542141#acquittal-and-resulting-riots.

14. Finally, all of you be of one mind, having compassion for one another; love as brothers, be tenderhearted, be courteous; not returning evil for evil or reviling for reviling, but on the contrary blessing, knowing that you were called to this, that you may inherit a blessing.
For "He who would love life
And see good days,
Let him refrain his tongue from evil,
And his lips from speaking deceit.
Let him turn away from evil and do good;
Let him seek peace and pursue it.
For the eyes of the LORD are on the righteous,
And His ears are open to their prayers;
But the face of the LORD is against those who do evil." (1 Peter 3:8-12)

15. "Bob Marley Quotes," BrainyQuote.com, accessed on March 10, 2017, https://www.brainyquote.com/quotes/quotes/b/bobmarley167094.html.

16. "Martin Luther King Jr. Quotes," BrainyQuote.com, accessed on March 10, 2017, https://www.brainyquote.com/quotes/quotes/m/martinluth101309.html.

Chapter 24 – Competition

1. "Definition of Competition," Merriam-Webster Dictionary, accessed on January 30, 2016, http://www.merriam-webster.com/dictionary/competition.

2. Be strong and of good courage, do not fear nor be afraid of them; for the LORD your God, He is the One who goes with you. He will not leave you nor forsake you. (Deuteronomy 31:6)

3. Be diligent to present yourself approved to God, a worker who does not need to be ashamed, rightly dividing the word of truth. (2 Timothy 2:15)

4. "These 8 Men are richer than 3.6 billion people combined," CNN Money, accessed on March 18, 2017, http://money.cnn.com/2017/01/15/news/economy/oxfam-income-inequality-men/.

5. "Checking Bernie Sanders on Americans' low voter-turnout rate," Politifact, accessed on March 18, 2017, http://www.politifact.com/truth-o-meter/statements/2015/apr/02/bernie-s/checking-bernie-sanders-americans-low-voter-turnou/.

6. "Franklin D. Roosevelt Quotes," BrainyQuote.com, accessed on March 23, 2017, https://www.brainyquote.com/quotes/authors/f/franklin_d_roosevelt.html.

7. And the LORD God formed man of the dust of the ground, and breathed into his nostrils the breath of life; and man became a living being. (Genesis 2:7)

8. Then Jacob was left alone; and a Man wrestled with him until the breaking of day. Now when He saw that He did not prevail against him, He touched the socket of his hip; and the socket of Jacob's hip was out of joint as He wrestled with him. And He said, "Let Me go, for the day breaks." But he said, "I will not let You go unless You bless me!" So He said to him, "What is your name?" He said, "Jacob." And He said, "Your name shall no longer be called Jacob, but Israel; for you have struggled with God and with men, and have prevailed." Then Jacob asked, saying, "Tell me Your name, I pray." And He said, "Why is it that you ask about My name?" And He blessed him there. (Genesis 32:24-29)

9. For we do not wrestle against flesh and blood, but against principalities, against powers, against the rulers of the darkness of this age, against spiritual hosts of wickedness in the heavenly places. Therefore take up the whole armor of God, that you may be able to withstand in the evil day, and having done all, to stand. (Ephesians 6:12-13)

10. Do you not know that those who run in a race all run, but one receives the prize? Run in such a way that you may obtain it. And everyone who competes for the prize is temperate in all things. Now they do it to obtain a perishable crown, but we for an imperishable crown. Therefore I run thus: not with uncertainty. Thus I fight: not as one who beats the air. But I discipline my body and bring it into subjection, lest, when I have preached to others, I myself should become disqualified. (1 Corinthians 9:24-27)

11. The LORD our God, the LORD is one! You shall love the LORD your God with all your heart, with all your soul, and with all your strength. (Deuteronomy 6:4-5)

12. And you shall remember the Lord your God, for it is He who gives you power to get wealth, that He may establish His covenant which He swore to your fathers, as it is this day. Then it shall be, if you by any means forget the Lord your God, and follow other gods, and serve them and worship them, I testify against you this day that you shall surely perish. As the nations which the Lord destroys before you, so you shall perish, because you would not be obedient to the voice of the Lord your God. (Deuteronomy 8:18-20)

13. How hard it is for those who have riches to enter the kingdom of God! For it is easier for a camel to go through the eye of a needle than for a rich man to enter the kingdom of God. (Luke 18:24-25)

Chapter 25 – Attraction

1. "Definition of Attraction," Merriam-Webster Dictionary, accessed on February 4, 2016, http://www.merriam-webster.com/dictionary/attraction.

2. Ask, and it will be given to you; seek, and you will find; knock, and it will be opened to you. For everyone who asks receives, and he who seeks finds, and to him who knocks it will be opened. (Matthew 7:7-8)

3. Who led you through that great and terrible wilderness, in which were fiery serpents and scorpions and thirsty land where there was no water; who brought water for you out of the flinty rock; who fed you in the wilderness with manna, which your fathers did not know, that He might humble you and that He might test you, to do you good in the end. (Deuteronomy 8:15-16)

4. "Maya Angelou Quotes," BrainyQuote.com, accessed on April 8, 2017, https://www.brainyquote.com/quotes/authors/m/maya_angelou.html.

5. Do not be deceived, God is not mocked; for whatever a man sows, that he will also reap. (Galatians 6:7)

6. And we know that all things work together for good to those who love God, to those who are the called according to His purpose. (Romans 8:28)

7. Great is our Lord, and mighty in power; His understanding is infinite. (Psalm 147:5)

8.   And Jesus came and spoke to them, saying, "All authority has been given to Me in heaven and on earth. Go therefore and make disciples of all the nations, baptizing them in the name of the Father and of the Son and of the Holy Spirit, teaching them to observe all things that I have commanded you; and lo, I am with you always, even to the end of the age." Amen. (Matthew 28:18-20)

9.   Yet in all these things we are more than conquerors through Him who loved us. For I am persuaded that neither death nor life, nor angels nor principalities nor powers, nor things present nor things to come, nor height nor depth, nor any other created thing, shall be able to separate us from the love of God which is in Christ Jesus our Lord. (Romans 8:37-39)

10. He is the image of the invisible God, the firstborn over all creation. For by Him all things were created that are in heaven and that are on earth, visible and invisible, whether thrones or dominions or principalities or powers. All things were created through Him and for Him. And He is before all things, and in Him all things consist. And He is the head of the body, the church, who is the beginning, the firstborn from the dead, that in all things He may have the preeminence. (Colossians 1:15-18)

Chapter 26 – Love

1.   "Definition of Love," Merriam-Webster Dictionary, accessed on February 8, 2016, http://www.merriam-webster.com/dictionary/love.

2.   But the fruit of the Spirit is love, joy, peace, longsuffering, kindness, goodness, faithfulness, gentleness, self-control. (Galatians 5:22-23)

3.   Jesus answered him, "The first of all the commandments is: 'Hear, O Israel, the LORD our God, the LORD is one. And you shall love the LORD your God with all your heart, with all your soul, with all your mind, and with all your strength.' This is the first commandment. And the second, like it, is this: 'You shall love your neighbor as yourself.' There is no other commandment greater than these." (Mark 12:29-31)

4.   Then God said, "Let Us make man in Our image, according to Our likeness; let them have dominion over the fish of the sea, over the birds of the air, and over the cattle, over all the earth and over every creeping thing that creeps on the earth." (Genesis 1:26)

5. Then the LORD God took the man and put him in the garden of Eden to tend and keep it. (Genesis 2:15)

6. The nations were angry, and Your wrath has come,
And the time of the dead, that they should be judged,
And that You should reward Your servants the prophets and the saints,
And those who fear Your name, small and great,
And should destroy those who destroy the earth. (Revelation 11:18)

7. A righteous man regards the life of his animal, But the tender mercies of the wicked are cruel. (Proverbs 12:10)

8. Be diligent to know the state of your flocks, and attend to your herds; for riches are not forever, nor does a crown endure to all generations. (Proverbs 27:23-24)

9. But I say to you who hear: Love your enemies, do good to those who hate you, bless those who curse you, and pray for those who spitefully use you. To him who strikes you on the one cheek, offer the other also. And from him who takes away your cloak, do not withhold your tunic either. Give to everyone who asks of you. And from him who takes away your goods do not ask them back. And just as you want men to do to you, you also do to them likewise. But if you love those who love you, what credit is that to you? For even sinners love those who love them. And if you do good to those who do good to you, what credit is that to you? For even sinners do the same. And if you lend to those from whom you hope to receive back, what credit is that to you? For even sinners lend to sinners to receive as much back. But love your enemies, do good, and lend, hoping for nothing in return; and your reward will be great, and you will be sons of the Most High. For He is kind to the unthankful and evil. Therefore, be merciful, just as your Father also is merciful. (Luke 6:27-36)

10. The days of our lives are seventy years; and if by reason of strength they are eighty years. (Psalm 90:10)

11. After this Job lived one hundred and forty years, and saw his children and grandchildren for four generations. So Job died, old and full of days. (Job 42:16-17)

12. Most men will proclaim each his own goodness, but who can find a faithful

man? The righteous man walks in his integrity; his children are blessed after him. (Proverbs 20:6-7)

13. He who finds a wife finds a good thing, and obtains favor from the LORD. (Proverbs 18:22)

14. Houses and riches are an inheritance from fathers, but a prudent wife is from the LORD. (Proverbs 19:14)

15. For this reason a man shall leave his father and mother and be joined to his wife, and the two shall become one flesh. (Ephesians 5:31)

16. Owe no one anything except to love one another, for he who loves another has fulfilled the law. For the commandments, "You shall not commit adultery," "You shall not murder," "You shall not steal," "You shall not bear false witness," "You shall not covet," and if there is any other commandment, are all summed up in this saying, namely, "You shall love your neighbor as yourself." Love does no harm to a neighbor; therefore love is the fulfillment of the law. (Romans 13:8-10)

17. My little children, let us not love in word or in tongue, but in deed and in truth. (1 John 3:18)

18. Though I speak with the tongues of men and of angels, but have not love, I have become sounding brass or a clanging cymbal. And though I have the gift of prophecy, and understand all mysteries and all knowledge, and though I have all faith, so that I could remove mountains, but have not love, I am nothing. And though I bestow all my goods to feed the poor, and though I give my body to be burned, but have not love, it profits me nothing. Love suffers long and is kind; love does not envy; love does not parade itself, is not puffed up; does not behave rudely, does not seek its own, is not provoked, thinks no evil; does not rejoice in iniquity, but rejoices in the truth; bears all things, believes all things, hopes all things, endures all things. Love never fails. But whether there are prophecies, they will fail; whether there are tongues, they will cease; whether there is knowledge, it will vanish away. For we know in part and we prophesy in part. But when that which is perfect has come, then that which is in part will be done away. When I was a child, I spoke as a child, I understood as a child, I thought as a child; but when I became a man, I put away childish things. For now we see in a mirror, dimly, but then face to face. Now I know in part, but then I shall know just as I

also am known. And now abide faith, hope, love, these three; but the greatest of these is love. (1 Corinthians 13:1-13)

19. There is no fear in love; but perfect love casts out fear. (1 John 4:18)

Chapter 27 – Sex

1. "Definition of Sex," Merriam-Webster Dictionary, accessed on February 10, 2016, http://www.merriam-webster.com/dictionary/sex.

2. Enoch lived sixty-five years, and begot Methuselah. After he begot Methuselah, Enoch walked with God three hundred years, and had sons and daughters. So all the days of Enoch were three hundred and sixty-five years. And Enoch walked with God; and he was not, for God took him. (Genesis 5:21-24)

3. And so it was, when they had crossed over, that Elijah said to Elisha, "Ask! What may I do for you, before I am taken away from you?" Elisha said, "Please let a double portion of your spirit be upon me." So he said, "You have asked a hard thing. Nevertheless, if you see me when I am taken from you, it shall be so for you; but if not, it shall not be so." Then it happened, as they continued on and talked, that suddenly a chariot of fire appeared with horses of fire, and separated the two of them; and Elijah went up by a whirlwind into heaven. (2 Kings 2:9-11)

4. Now when He had spoken these things, while they watched, He was taken up, and a cloud received Him out of their sight. And while they looked steadfastly toward heaven as He went up, behold, two men stood by them in white apparel, who also said, "Men of Galilee, why do you stand gazing up into heaven? This same Jesus, who was taken up from you into heaven, will so come in like manner as you saw Him go into heaven." (Acts 1:9-11)

5. The word of the LORD also came to me, saying, "You shall not take a wife, nor shall you have sons or daughters in this place." (Jeremiah 16:1-2)

6. "Definition of Reproduction," Merriam-Webster Dictionary, accessed on April 11, 2017, https://www.merriam-webster.com/dictionary/reproduction.

7. "Definition of Procreate," Merriam-Webster Dictionary, accessed April 11, 2107, https://www.merriam-webster.com/dictionary/procreation.

8. So God created man in His own image; in the image of God He created him; male and female He created them. Then God blessed them, and God said to them, "Be fruitful and multiply; fill the earth and subdue it; have dominion over the fish of the sea, over the birds of the air, and over every living thing that moves on the earth." (Genesis 1:27-28)

9. Marriage is honorable among all, and the bed undefiled; but fornicators and adulterers God will judge. (Hebrews 13:4)

10. Nevertheless, because of sexual immorality, let each man have his own wife, and let each woman have her own husband. Let the husband render to his wife the affection due her, and likewise also the wife to her husband. The wife does not have authority over her own body, but the husband does. And likewise the husband does not have authority over his own body, but the wife does. Do not deprive one another except with consent for a time, that you may give yourselves to fasting and prayer; and come together again so that Satan does not tempt you because of your lack of self-control. (1 Corinthians 7:2-5)

11. Or do you not know that he who is joined to a harlot is one body with her? For "the two," He says, "shall become one flesh." But he who is joined to the Lord is one spirit with Him. Flee sexual immorality. Every sin that a man does is outside the body, but he who commits sexual immorality sins against his own body. Or do you not know that your body is the temple of the Holy Spirit who is in you, whom you have from God, and you are not your own? For you were bought at a price; therefore glorify God in your body and in your spirit, which are God's. (1 Corinthians 6:16-20)

12. "The Power of Touch," Healthy Living, AARP, accessed on April 12, 2017, http://www.aarp.org/health/healthy-living/info-2015/power-of-touch.html.

13. For this reason God gave them up to vile passions. For even their women exchanged the natural use for what is against nature. Likewise also the men, leaving the natural use of the woman, burned in their lust for one another, men with men committing what is shameful, and receiving in themselves the penalty of their error which was due. And even as they did not like to retain God in their knowledge, God gave them over to a debased mind, to do those things which are not fitting; being filled with all unrighteousness, sexual immorality, wickedness, covetousness, maliciousness; full of envy, murder, strife, deceit, evil-mindedness; they are whisperers, backbiters, haters of God, violent, proud, boasters, inventors

of evil things, disobedient to parents, undiscerning, untrustworthy, unloving, unforgiving, unmerciful; who, knowing the righteous judgment of God, that those who practice such things are deserving of death, not only do the same but also approve of those who practice them. (Romans 1:26-32)

14. Drink water from your own cistern,
And running water from your own well.
Should your fountains be dispersed abroad,
Streams of water in the streets?
Let them be only your own,
And not for strangers with you.
Let your fountain be blessed,
And rejoice with the wife of your youth.
As a loving deer and a graceful doe,
Let her breasts satisfy you at all times;
And always be enraptured with her love.
For why should you, my son, be enraptured by an immoral woman,
And be embraced in the arms of a seductress? (Proverbs 5:15-20)

15. Two are better than one,
Because they have a good reward for their labor.
For if they fall, one will lift up his companion.
But woe to him who is alone when he falls,
For he has no one to help him up.
Again, if two lie down together, they will keep warm;
But how can one be warm alone?
Though one may be overpowered by another, two can withstand him.
And a threefold cord is not quickly broken. (Ecclesiastes 4:9-12)

16. Therefore if you have not been faithful in the unrighteous mammon, who will commit to your trust the true riches? (Luke 16:11)